The Speed Mushing Manual

How to Train Racing Sled Dogs

by

Jim Welch

Sirius Publishing
Eagle River, Alaska

ACKNOWLEDGEMENTS

Thanks to all the people and dogs who taught me the lessons contained in this book. Most I have neglected to mention by name, but I am forever grateful nonetheless.

I thank especially those who allowed this project to reach the printed page. Jim Harvey, Andy Perala, Devony Lehner, and Bella Levorsen made editorial suggestions.

Paul McCormick, Lisa Fallgren Stevens, Bill Sherwonnit, Eric Hill, Michael Penn, and John Hotzfield provided photographs. The Anchorage Times, The Anchorage Daily News and Arner Publications gave permission to reprint photographs.

Michelle Cusick, Nancy Veitch, Matt Cusick and Richard Eathorne generously gave their effort and expertise in the design and technical realization of the book.

I am indebted to Mary Shields, Shannon Cartwright and the people of MUSHING magazine for their advice and Arner Publications for permission to quote from *Everything I Know About Training and Racing Sled Dogs* by George Attla. Finally I thank Bob Levorsen for his support throughout. - *J.P.W.*

Copyright © 1989 by James P. Welch. All rights reserved. No part of this book may be reproduced or transmitted in any form or by any means, electronic or mechanical, including photocopying, recording or by any information storage and retrieval system without written permission from the author, except for the inclusion of brief quotations in a review.

First Edition 1989

Library of Congress Catalog Card Number 89-91976

ISBN 0-9623643-0-4

Cover photo of Jim Welch by Paul McCormick
Cover Design by Nancy Veitch, Book Design by Michelle Cusick
Printed in the U.S.A

Sirius Publishing
P.O. Box 770404
Eagle River, Alaska 99577

"The surest thing there is is we are riders,
   And though none to successful at it, guiders..."

- Robert Frost

The author and "Groucho" after winning the 1986 Eagle River Classic.
Photo by Bill Sherwonnit for The Anchorage Times

TABLE OF CONTENTS

Introduction 7
    NIGHTMARE ON HUSKY STREET

Chapter One 11
    AXIOMS FOR A DOG MUSHER

Chapter Two 17
    BUILDING A GOOD DOG TEAM - Dog Characteristics... Buying Good Dogs... Buying vs. Breeding... Breeding: When the Time Comes... Successful Breeders... Other Breeding Permutations

Chapter Three 37
    FEED 'EM GOOD - Dietary Balance... Preparation of Foods... Dietary Supplements... Water... Dehydration... Charlies's Race Diet

Chapter Four 47
    ELEMENTS OF CONDITIONING - Strength... Endurance... Speed... Balance, Agility and Neuromuscular Coordination... Summary

Chapter Five 55
    ELEMENTS OF TRAINING - A Training Outline... Cues and Commands... Trained To Do What?... Training and Age... Puppies... Yearlings... Adults

Chapter Six 67
    CONDITIONING AND TRAINING: PUTTING IT ALL TOGETHER - Cart Training Equipment... Fall Cart Training... Late Fall... Early Winter

Chapter Seven 85
    SPEED - December and Beyond: Getting Fit, Getting Fast... Basic Pace... Conditioning for Speed... Intervals... Speed Response Training... Trained Insistence... Race Ready... Some Additional Thoughts on Training

Chapter Eight 107
   EQUIPMENT: THE RIGHT TOOLS FOR THE JOB - In the Dog Lot... On the Trail... On the Dog... Equipment for Race Day

Chapter Nine 121
   RACE - THE GAMES, THE WARS - Playing the Game, Fighting the War ... "Psych Out"... The Race Focus

INTRODUCTION

"Nightmare on Husky Street"

When I first decided to take sled dog racing seriously, I did some homework. I went to races and I looked at lots of dogs. I went to club meetings, talked to dog drivers and read everything I could find. Then I took the plunge and bought five dogs from George Attla. I paid $3000. It was a big bite but I planned to have serious fun.

Before that I had worked with my pet dogs. I taught them how to pull a sled and pretend they were sled dogs. But the dogs from George Attla were genuine racing huskies. I had confidence in these dogs. But I had a lot to learn and no idea what they would soon put me through.

Shortly after I brought the dogs home, my father flew to Alaska to visit. He wanted to take some home movies of the dogs in action. He had no idea what to expect. Unfortunately, neither did I. We got out the wheeled training rig, the new ganglines and harnesses and began to hook up the dogs for our maiden voyage. As each dog was harnessed, the frenzy mounted. They were loud and they were eager, jumping, lunging, screaming to go. I played the role of great Alaskan dog musher for my father. He hollered, "ACTION," and the camera began to roll.

Just as I snapped the last dog into the team, the towline suddenly broke right ahead of the wheeled rig. My brand new dog team shot down the road, leaving me stranded at the truck like a bride left waiting at the altar.

It is every dog musher's nightmare. Visions flashed through my mind, a lost dog team - tangled, struggling, dying dogs. In a matter of seconds hundreds of horrible possibilities bombarded my imagination. I chased the runaway team with everything I had, gasping in the wake of their dust.

I ran down the gravel road for half a mile, stumbling and gasping, but soon lost sight of them. Then, incredibly, miraculously, a dog team appeared on the horizon. A moving mass of dogs was charging straight toward me. Sparky, *my* big, brown, flop - footed, trapline leader from Allakaket had turned the team around and was leading them back, full speed ahead.

To anyone who knows dog teams, this is the stuff of fairy tales and fantasy movies, not real life. A leader might turn a hard running team around for Jack London or Sergeant Preston, but certainly not for me. Every dog musher eventually loses hold of his dog team. I had lost mine the first time out. Fortunately, George Attla sold me a leader who knew more than I did about running a dog team. And so began the lessons these dogs would teach me.

Many years, many dogs, and many races since, I still remember things these five dogs taught me that no human ever could. Sparky taught me what a tough headed dog will do despite physical limitations. Florence showed me how powerfully and smoothly an athletically gifted dog can run. And Quick, a nine month old pup when I bought him, taught me that although leaders may be developed, the really good ones are born, not made. Quick would later become my first and best Rendezvous leader and the sire of many fine dogs.

This book is intended for people who want to become better dog mushers and drive faster dog teams. It is not a "complete guide of all-you-need-to-know." It is compiled from research, hands on experience, and the words and deeds of dog mushers I have known. George Attla, Gareth Wright, Charlie Champaine, Harvey Drake, Doc Lombard, Harris Dunlap and many more taught me important lessons. I hope the reader will find some of the information I pass on helpful in becoming a better dog musher, or simply as a reminder of things best not forgotten.

After all these years I still cannot say I understand the compulsion of driving sled dogs. For those affected, dog mushing is a powerful addiction. Iditarod musher Dewey Halverson told me he would have been better off with heroin; it would have been cheaper and less addictive.

I never intended to become as immersed as I did. But, things change. And if you didn't already know, I warn you, nothing will satisfy that compulsion like a ride down the trail behind a fast dog team.

While fundamental principles of training and racing may not change, our ability to apply those principles does. There is more information available to a dog driver today than even 10 years ago. For example, we now know that feeding a standard commercial dry dog food is not optimal for high level competition. We have seen the increased number of races and the wide variety of distances alter basic conditioning strategies and tactics in the management of a team.

George Attla, who is the most prolific race winner of all time, trains quite differently today than when he wrote his book *Everything I Know About Training and Racing Sled Dogs*, more than 15 years ago. His gangline measurements, snow hook design, feed ingredients, and training schedules are all different today. The Fur Rendezvous World Championship Race in Anchorage has even changed and so have training preparations for it. We now have far more races with far greater demands on speed at all distances than ever before.

Most of these developments aren't readily accessible in print. I learned to drive dogs in this time period. I learned about these improvements through experience, feedback, and the words and example of the world's best dog mushers.

There are many people who know far more than I about training, managing, and racing sled dogs. There are also far more gifted and successful trainers. And there are a lot more people who will make sure that I remember it, because I live in Alaska, which is home to the best of them.

There are also a few really good books available. But for the most part, those who know more haven't been interested or willing to write about it. Most of the information in this book did not start with me. It is simply information and experience from people that I feel will prove worthwhile to you in your efforts to become a better dog musher.

I have tried to give credit to some of the people I have learned from or who have publicly made an effort to spread helpful information to people who want to become better dog drivers. I have undoubtedly left out many very important people and sources of valuable knowledge and information. I hope this will suffice for an apology.

No one can give you a prescription for success. Many of the tidbits in this book are so taken for granted by veterans, that I think most wouldn't even consciously think to mention them. Some I hope, will make your ride faster.

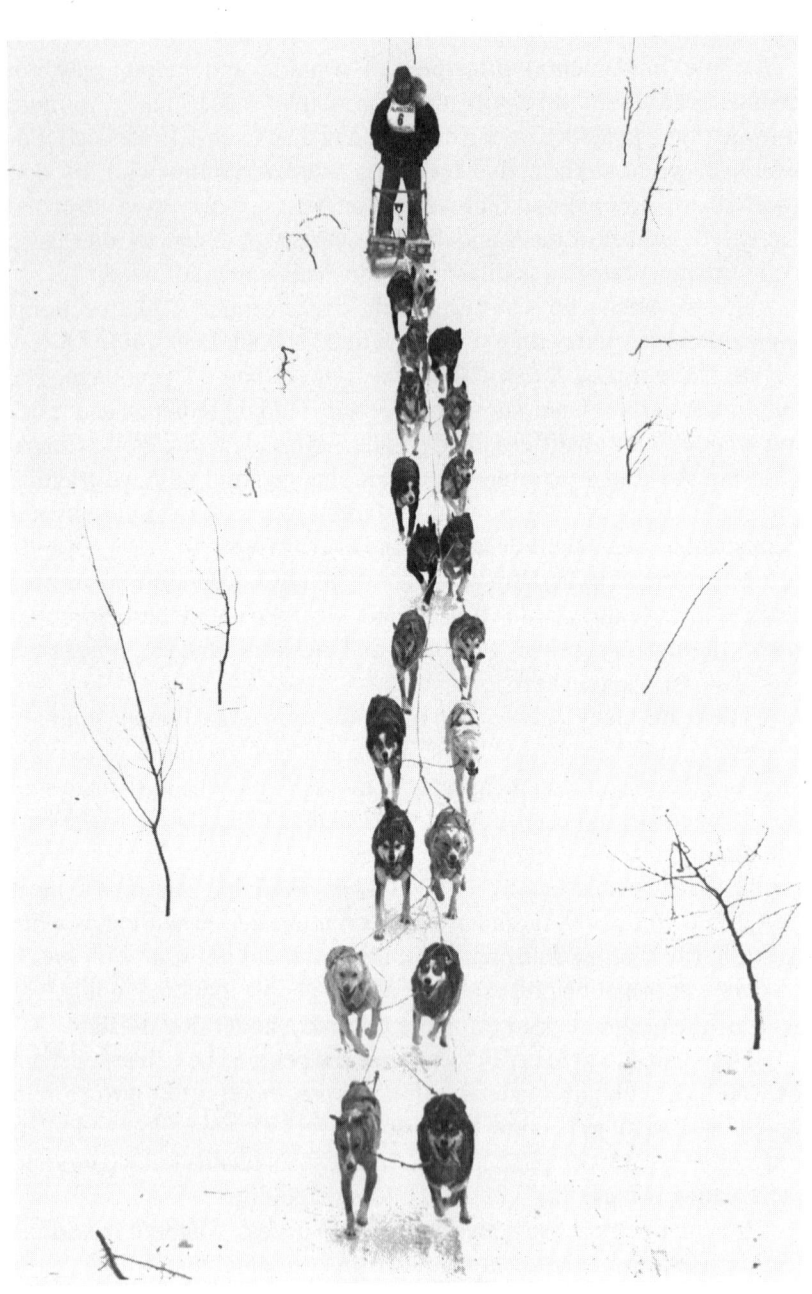

Marvin Kokrine putting everything together to win the 1988 North American Championship. *Photo by Lisa Fallgren Stevens*

Chapter 1
Axioms For A Dog Musher

I believe there are three essential axioms to becoming a good dog musher.

Axiom # 1

"Learn Wherever And Whenever You Can"

This means keeping your ears open 100% of the time and mouth closed 90% of the time. It means listening constantly for information that may be relevant to your own dog team. It means evaluating and learning from your own daily experience with your dogs.

I remember watching the North American Championship (held each March in Fairbanks) early in my career from the bridge crossing the Chena River. Two experienced mushers, Denis Christman and Bobby Lee were with me. We were all watching the same teams from the same perspective and yet I couldn't understand how these guys could notice so much detail in a string of sixteen dogs flying by.

They seemed able to pick out each individual dog and describe how it was performing. "Look at the dog on the right behind swing. He's really smooth," or "that black dog ahead of wheel is crippled and the one ahead of him will never make it tomorrow." All I saw was a blur.

It was only after watching thousands of teams later that my eye developed enough to be able to see a team as a unit and instantly

The Speed Mushing Manual

recognize the standouts and the weak links, to see the stride length and gaits of all the dogs as they fit in that unit.

During the Fur Rendezvous World Championships each February in Anchorage, we videotape the TV coverage and watch tapes made from specific places on the trail. Like watching the game films of professional sports teams, you want to assess strengths and weaknesses of the competitors.

Though I have learned from champions as well as novices, I have tried to test information I have gotten even from people whose knowledge I respect. I do this not only to verify, but to see if and how that knowledge can be applied to my style and my dogs. Although Axiom # 1 says, "Learn Whenever and Wherever You Can", you must realize that your own good judgement must always be applied since you

Clyde Mayo
Photo by Paul McCormick

Axioms For A Dog Musher

will often find more dog manure in a mushing conversation than in any dog lot.

You can learn most from good drivers, good dogs, and lots of experience. You can learn from a lot of other sources, but without association with these three, you will eventually come to a standstill.

One of the best situations to learn is after a race. At any race, the crowd will be at the winner's truck. This adulation is well deserved, but don't forget the others who might be the winner tomorrow, and how less crowded it is at the cuff of his (and remember that also means her) pants.

Clyde Mayo, after nearly winning the Rendezvous in 1982 (when he finished second), experienced disappointing seasons in 1983 and 1984. He related to me how fickle his fame and his followers had been. After doing so well in 1982, people came to him in droves offering to help, to handle for him, and be involved with his whole endeavor. By the spring of '84 he had great difficulty in even finding a handler and was quite candid about the fact that no one came around any more with offers of help.

Charlie Champaine's leader, Bruce, was the kingpin of his team for years of solid top notch racing. But it was not until Charlie's phenomenal season in 1984 when he won every race he entered except one (where his team became tangled in a nylon fence) including the Fur Rendezvous World Championship at Anchorage, that people began streaming to his doorstep to breed their females to Bruce. While he was properly gratified, he felt it ironic that Bruce was only being "discovered" after his final season as main leader.

George Attla once said that if he gave his lead dog a cigarette after the race, by the following week he would see at least ten cigarettes hanging out of various dogs' mouths in other teams. While it is certain that a lot can and should be learned from the champion, it is important to remember that they learned the hard lessons long before.

Everybody wants a piece of the champion - a small favor here, a special secret there, a good dog at a cheap price. Certainly one reason why champions are items of such immense interest and curiosity is that people are looking for the secrets and formulas for their success. A certain reticence at this onslaught is understandable.

But champions are made well before the race is won and these future champions can be tremendous sources of information not likely to be found out from the winner. In many respects I believe that a

The Speed Mushing Manual

champion is trying to learn how to remain a champion while "mere mortals" are concerned with the far different issue of getting there.

George Attla
"If I gave my lead dog a cigarette after the race, by the following week I'd see at least ten cigarettes hanging out of other dogs' mouths." *Photo by Paul McCormick*

Axioms For A Dog Musher

But "how to get there" is often much more hungrily and daringly pursued by those on the threshold. Though the champions hold immense knowledge, they have already left behind many of the issues I am addressing here, namely, how to get the knowledge, information, experience, and dogs to become a good dog musher. The "thresholders" can talk candidly, because often nobody listens to what they have to say anyway.

Axiom # 2

"Place Yourself In A Position Where You Have The Opportunity To Learn"

Good dogs and good dog drivers tend to go together, so where you find one, you are likely to find the other. Go to meetings, go to races, introduce yourself to drivers, offer to help someone that lives nearby, read everything you can, do everything you can with dogs to know dogs better. Drive dogs for miles and miles. Dogs cannot learn everything at once. The same is true for the driver. Look hard at good dogs and good methods. The key lies in building your own experience and assimilating everything you learn.

I live in Alaska, where I am surrounded by good dog drivers, good dogs and the opportunity to be thoroughly involved with driving dogs. But geographical location is only part of it. Just as important is a position that allows you communication opportunities and experience from which to learn. I progressed only because I sought out those who can teach. I observed and gradually acquired good dogs. To acquire my experience I have driven dog teams thousands of miles.

I came here specifically to place myself in a position where I could have the opportunity to learn. That was my answer. There are many others, in far less exotic places than Alaska. What counts is having a plan that will allow you to learn.

Axiom # 3

"Act Upon What You Learn"

All the knowledge in the world accomplishes nothing unless its translated into action. Many people make a career of saying they want

The Speed Mushing Manual

to grow and improve, get better performance from their team, but nonetheless seem unable to progress. They talk but don't act. They are not really willing to do what it takes. Grumblers and procrastinators do not good dog mushers make.

Get good dogs and spend as much time with them as possible. A good dog will teach you things that a mediocre dog cannot. You can never go faster than the quality of your dogs allow, although most people never come close to approaching the limits of the dogs they own. Nonetheless, while it is a cheap lesson to make most of your rudimentary mistakes on less expensive dogs, a good dog can teach you things that you can learn no other way.

Most people never really get to ride behind a really super dog. Many I know will argue that they have, but most simply haven't seen what they are missing. It is a humbling experience to have your preconceptions shattered. A good one will spoil you, but should help raise your standards. It unfortunately will make you less satisfied with everything else you own.

Spend time with your dogs. Clean up after them, brush them, rough house with them, feed them, interact with them. Be the focal point of their social unit. Know your dogs and what makes them tick, what makes them run and what makes them fly.

Notice that of the seven dogs in the picture, only three feet are touching the ground. This is as close to flying as it gets. Leaders are Quick (Black dog) and Gusto. *Photo by Al Cronk*

Chapter 2
Building A Good Dog Team

DOG CHARACTERISTICS

A good dog team is a lot more fun to drive than a mediocre one, and the only way to build a good dog team is to get good dogs. Building a good dog team, whether you are starting from scratch or trying to improve the quality of team you already have, requires some forethought and some homework. Acquiring dogs is easy, especially those that nobody else wants, but it takes a little more knowledge and effort to acquire good dogs.

Take some time to look hard at good dogs, not the neighborhood show dog or the culls of a friend of a friend, but dogs that are winning races. Notice what they look like, which muscles seem most developed, the proportions of the body, the angles that legs and feet connect with the rest of the body, how they act, how they perform, what their gait looks like, and where they come from.

Ask the driver which is his best dog and ask him to describe the features of the dog he likes best. Ask him what are the dog's weaknesses, and could he illustrate it by comparing it to another dog on the scene. Many top dog drivers would be hard pressed to articulate the specifics they look for when describing a well built dog, but they could point one out in an instant. Many have learned to judge a dog from the lessons given them by the top drivers that preceded them and by looking closely at thousands of dogs.

A dog in top shape should have hard musculature, especially along the back and the thigh. The stomach muscles should be hard and corded. I have learned to look for a long humerus bone (the bone between the elbow and shoulder of the front leg) and a rounded stifle and croup. Long tibia and fibula bones in the rear legs are desirable for speed as

The Speed Mushing Manual

long as they are balanced by the rest of the body. I want the muscles of the shoulders and thighs to be long from front to back rather than small or bulging.

Some of this will of course depend on what type of conditioning the dog has been involved in and what time of year it is. A dog that has been trained for distance trotting will develop an entirely different look than the same dog trained and conditioned to run fast. Be careful not to confuse the type or lack of conditioning with structural or musculature faults. A careful eye, however, will be able to make the distinction between a race dog and an Edsel.

Dogs that are really well built appear very non descript to the casual observer. Dogs that stand out to the spectator because of tremendously long legs or long body or any other bodily extremes usually do not stand out at the finish line of a tough race. Extremely short coupled dogs will have no speed. Extremely long dogs may be fast but will have little

"Marvin" - (Nerds x Florence)
Bred by the author, a beautifully built dog now owned by Susan Wagnon in Anchorage. *Photo by Michael Penn for The Anchorage Daily News*

endurance. I have seen dogs like that do very well in short (10 mile) races, but they always seem to pay the toll in longer races like the Rendezvous or the North American.

I like dogs with a relatively high tuck up in the waist without seeming pinched or extreme. This trait comes from the hound bred into the lines decades ago by Gareth Wright and others. If you look at pictures of any dogs noted for speed, they share this trait. The gentle rounding of the hind end is something George pointed out years ago and remains very desirable. It is an indication of a pelvic structure angled best for efficient striding.

If you can observe a dog run, all the better. Very few people will allow you try a dog out before purchasing (understandably so) but some may offer to take you along in the basket or on a second sled to show you the dog in action. How any given dog acts the first time he is hooked up with strange dogs in front of a strange driver is not necessarily

"Penguin" - (Quick x Snowball)
One of Quick's exceptionally well built pups, bred by the author, now owned by Magnar Aasheim in Norway.

indicative of how the dog will perform for you later. But placed in a familiar context with the driver the dog knows will show you a lot.

You may not see the upper end of his speed because you are traveling with two people. You probably won't have the opportunity to see the limit of the dog's endurance either because the run has to suit the particular needs of the owner's training program at that time. What you can observe is the dogs attitude toward working, the status of his tugline, and the kind of gait the dog runs with.

Ideally, a gait should be as smooth as a polished bullet, with all motion directed forward. There should be little or no up and down movement. I had the opportunity to drive a top notch dog very early in my career. She was a dog named Florence and if I was a sailor, I would probably have her name tattooed on my arm. She was the smoothest running and the most athletically talented dog I have ever run. I swear that if you balanced a glass of water on her back during a run that she would not spill a drop during the whole run. Watching her was perhaps the single most valuable lesson I have ever had in dog mushing. I saw what a good dog can do.

A smooth gaited dog does not appear to be working very hard, but the tug line will tell the story. A good dog will have a tug line that never slacks. It should be as straight as a laser beam. If it is tight all the time, the dog is working right. An ideal dog team will have dogs with the same "jump" or stride length. This will ultimately determine how fast and how far a team can really function as a unit. Look for the tug line to be tight when the dog jumps into a stride as well as when he lands. The truth is in the tug.

Avoid dogs with a tight curl in their tail or with necks too short. They will lack in speed. The tight curl is a defect, usually indicating vertebrae that are too close together. The short neck is an imbalance. Avoid very large dogs and very small dogs. I prefer males that are not much more than 50 pounds and females that are not smaller than 40 pounds, although I have had some very good ones that fell outside this range.

The larger dogs tend to ultimately have trouble with the distance, even if they are able to maintain an adequate speed. They are often very effective animals for shorter or limited class races because of their increased pulling power. They will lose speed at a younger age and in general seem more susceptible to injury. But the proof is in the perfor-

"Florence" - (Scotty x Peaches)
The white leader on driver's right, Florence in her prime - "... if you balanced a glass of water on her back during a run she would not spill a drop..." *Photo by Lisa Fallgren Stevens*

mance. If I had a 350 pound dog that could run the same speed and distance as the rest of the team, you can be sure it would be in my team.

The problem with a smaller dog is what you might expect, a lack of pulling power. In a big team, the importance of this diminishes, but it does shift a disproportionate amount of responsibility to the other dogs. Generally small size can be forgiven more if the dog is good enough to run near the front of the team and puts a lot on the line. But if a dog is under 40 pounds, it better have a lot on that line or be a leader, in which case, all is forgiven.

Though dogs that don't look like they are the right size and the right build can sometimes perform well, generally they can't and don't. The deck is stacked against them. If you plan to be in this game for long, a smart player sticks where the odds are best. In general, physical curiosities do not good odds make.

At least as important as any combination of physical characteristics is the mental makeup of the dog. Charlie Champaine says the most important part of the body is between the ears. I agree, especially when the going gets tough. Though a dog's confidence and security can be greatly influenced by his upbringing, mental toughness seems very heavily genetic and is a trait to examine carefully when selecting and breeding dogs.

BUYING GOOD DOGS

Depending on how much confidence you have in your own ability to judge a good dog, you may have to rely on an owner's opinion as well as a dog's performance record and pedigree as to how good a dog really is. An owner's opinion of a dog is only as valuable as your opinion of the owner, of course.

If you have doubts, talk to some people who have purchased dogs from that person before. Find out if the dog sold was represented fairly. It doesn't matter if the dog was the greatest as long as the representation was honest and the price commensurate with the ability of the dog.

Until you can judge a dog for yourself, you will have to depend on other's opinions, the performance record of the dog, and the ancestry of the dog. I believe, right from the start, a dog musher has got to acquaint himself with the lineages of top dogs and top teams. Most good dogs are somehow related, even if it is distantly, with several well developed strains or lines which have branched off and may now emphasize different qualities such as speed, attitude, endurance, tough mindedness.

Look at any winning team. With a little bit of questioning, you will probably find that the bulk of the team is related. By understanding the genetic relation of the team, you can begin to discern the type and character of different lines. Some lines are notorious for high attitude, - screaming, lunging, foaming to go. Some are known for running hard out of the chute with everything they've got until they collapse. Others are known to be calmer, more easily controlled, and tireless. Some lines have some serious genetic faults, such as retinal atrophy. Some are tough minded, while others have cream of wheat for brains.

J.P. Norris put out a pedigree of all the dogs participating in the North American Championship and has sold each year's edition at a very nominal price. When he took a break from this task, Jeff Conn, a Fairbanks musher, picked up where J.P. left off. This is a lot of very useful and valuable information and is really a tremendous service. This list would be a good introduction to the seminal lines and dogs prominent in dog racing. Dogs such as George Attla's Scotty and Harvey Drake's Junior (originally bred by Steve Losonsky) are examples of prepotent studs that have consistently sired many top quality dogs. This kind of information jumps from the pages of J.P.'s North American pedigree list.

For many years, if you wanted to know the background of a dog, you would have to talk to the breeder or someone very familiar with those specific lines. A few people, like Denis Christman or Steve and Rosie Losonsky, kept meticulous records and freely shared them with anyone who asked. Other very successful racers probably kept most of these backgrounds in their head, but their recall seemed to vary tremendously, depending who asked for the information.

Buying a dog with good background does not guarantee that a dog will be a good one, but the probability is so extraordinarily higher than that of a dog with poor or no proven background, that it simply does not make sense to ignore ancestry when purchasing a dog. In addition to the increased likelihood that the dog will be a good performer, it might improve potential for successful breeding.

It is certainly possible that a dog could be an excellent performer and have very unfamiliar background. A dog like this should not be ignored by any means. After all, performance is the standard of selection. However, the "gem" that comes from nowhere is more often a product of wishful thinking than genetic exception. If a dog really is an exceptional performer, grab it, but if a dog of equal ability that has a proven background is available, that dog is certainly preferred.

A seller can really make a dog sound impressive regardless of what level of competition the dog has performed in. Words like "that's the best I've ever run" or that's the "hardest working" or "fastest" or any number of superlatives can make potential buyers really open up their ears and their wallets. My favorite example is the guy who had been finishing twenty or thirty minutes behind the next to last finisher stated about one of his dogs, "they may not all be fast but that one is fast enough to go with anyone's team." Dick Tozier, long time race marshal in Anchorage, commented, "Even if it were true, HOW would he know?" The dog had never run in a team that could test his top speed.

Most often, the seller believes what he is saying and is probably telling the truth as he understands it. If he is beating you with that dog in his team or is doing well in more difficult competition than you, that may well be truth enough.

There are many dogs available that would make a lot of people very happy and improve their team markedly. Because that dog didn't quite make the winning Rendezvous team is no reason that it might not be a

The Speed Mushing Manual

Dick Tozier
Probably the best known and most highly respected Race Marshal in all of Dog Mushing. *Photo by Paul McCormick*

spectacular dog for you. The better your team gets, the harder it will become to buy dogs that will improve it. But as long as you can buy better dogs than you can reliably produce, do it. It is faster and cheaper than any other means.

BREEDING VERSUS BUYING

Any serious dog musher eventually ends up breeding dogs to replenish and improve his team. Before doing this, however, a guy needs to take a hard and honest look at what he's got to breed and how much it's going to cost compared to what can be acquired through other means. Someone who stays in dogs sooner or later will breed dogs, although it almost always should be later than sooner.

You cannot reliably expect to produce puppies better than the poorer of the parents. Puppies consume almost twice the amount of food that adults do, require numerous vaccinations, worming and veterinary involvement. At the time of this writing, Parvo virus is still a major mortality factor among pups. The cost of raising a litter until they are old enough to be fairly evaluated in harness is substantial. They also require an incredible amount of time, effort, and patience.

If you have a good team to start with, the percentage of pups who will be good enough to make your team will probably not be as high as you thought. In fact, the higher quality your team, the more selective the criteria for a young dog to make that team, hence the lower the percentage of pups that will ultimately make the team.

I recommend that you figure the total cost of raising six to eight pups for one year, then double it. You should now have a more accurate estimation of the true costs, and it should be a very substantial figure. Ask yourself, "Could I buy as good or better a dog than I could reasonably expect to come from this litter for that much money?" If the answer is "yes" or even "probably yes" then buy a dog and wait until you have better breeding stock. One good dog is worth one hundred mediocre dogs.

If you stay in dogs, you will eventually breed dogs, but as long as you can buy better dogs than you can breed, buy dogs. You will improve the overall quality of your team faster, hopefully improving the bloodlines in your lot so that your results will be better when you do breed. There is nothing sadder than seeing somebody acquire a few mediocre dogs and then before they even know what to look for, have twenty or thirty mediocre puppies on the ground.

Paying money up front for a good dog seems prohibitively expensive to many people, and for many it is. I am the last one to advise people to overextend themselves. However, I have never known any dog musher who regretted buying a good dog, regardless of the price. I know many people who spent good money trying to produce a good dog with nothing to show for it. Though the price tag of a good dog may seem high, it is usually far cheaper than what it would cost you to produce a dog of equal quality.

BREEDING: WHEN THE TIME COMES

There may finally come a time when the dogs you need are not for sale. If that's really true, then it means you must have a mighty good dog team, because pretty good dogs are always available for a price. Hopefully it means you have accumulated some dogs with proven bloodlines and you have educated yourself thoroughly about the lines of any dog you are considering breeding, have looked at the proven relatives and the breeding combinations that have shown proven results. You should certainly be able to recite pedigrees at least through grandparents and be familiar with the percentage of proven offspring.

I advise you to forget any exotic combinations or hybridizations. They have all been tried, from Greyhounds to poodles, wolves to sheepdogs, all in search of a super dog. People who have made improvements by introducing new elements have realized these gains only through a very elaborate and multi - generational program.

It is inevitably expensive, frustrating, and with far more failures than successes. People who have the "new" idea to cross a Greyhound with a Siberian to get speed X endurance are not dealing with a realistic venture. First, it has been tried many times. Second, it is just never that simple. If you go this route be prepared to eliminate many, many dogs in the process of attempting to arrive at something that looks and performs like a sled dog.

There are too many good lines of sled dogs available for anyone concerned with being competitive to chase some exotic breeding fantasy. It only makes sense to start with the best possible stock available. Even then, it is a long way to the top. There is no sense in needlessly handicapping yourself from the start.

There is much more to be learned from the success of others, simply from observation. Every new dog musher has the advantage of the body of knowledge accumulated and exemplified by the generations of drivers like the Wrights, the Attlas, Kokrines, Taylors, Redingtons and Erharts of the world. By example and by word, an immense body of knowledge has been made available to an entire generation of newcomers.

When I started my breeding program, I understood Mendelian genetics, and the standard AKC approach to breeding dogs. But the race is determined by who crosses the finish line with the fastest time. What I found far more useful was the program and example of people who were producing winning dog teams from their breeding. Those who have achieved performance results are doing something right, and that seems a logical place to start.

SUCCESSFUL BREEDERS

Most mushers would agree that if 25% of a litter can ultimately make a top team, you have achieved a very worthwhile breeding. In the late 70's George Attla had a run of breeding success that was nothing short of incredible. He bred five litters in the space of two years with well over 90% of the pups making either his team or other top teams. These litters were all sired by Scotty and bear some exceptional examples of breeding success. The dogs from these litters have continued to produce excellent progeny of their own.

I am choosing to focus on these particular dogs not only because of the dramatic success of the breedings and because I am very familiar with these particular lines, but because they represent the continuation of lines that can be traced back quite far and are well illustrated in the book George wrote with Bella Levorsen (*Everything I Know about Training and Racing Sled Dogs*). I think it might be interesting to look back at some of these well known dogs to see how George arrived at the breeding successes I have talked about by examining each dog, where it came from, what it produced and its relation to the other dogs.

I have chosen to focus on the first litter produced by Scotty x Freckles, and then follow the breeding patterns which attempted to continue and extend this exceptional litter. This breeding produced seven dogs, every one of which made George's team (one was sold as a pup and ran successfully on Peter Norberg's team). This breeding was later repeated with similar results. The next generation produced Tom, Prunes et al. followed by Pepy who was George's next main stud for a time.

Scotty was also bred to Freckles' littermate, Chris, with the same incredible results. For example, George's now retired main leader is Lingo, a Scotty x Chris pup that George has described as his best ever. (Lingo is the main stud at the Attla kennel at this writing, but to look at how George constructed his breeding sequence we need to look further down the line.)

But first, the pedigrees:

The Speed Mushing Manual

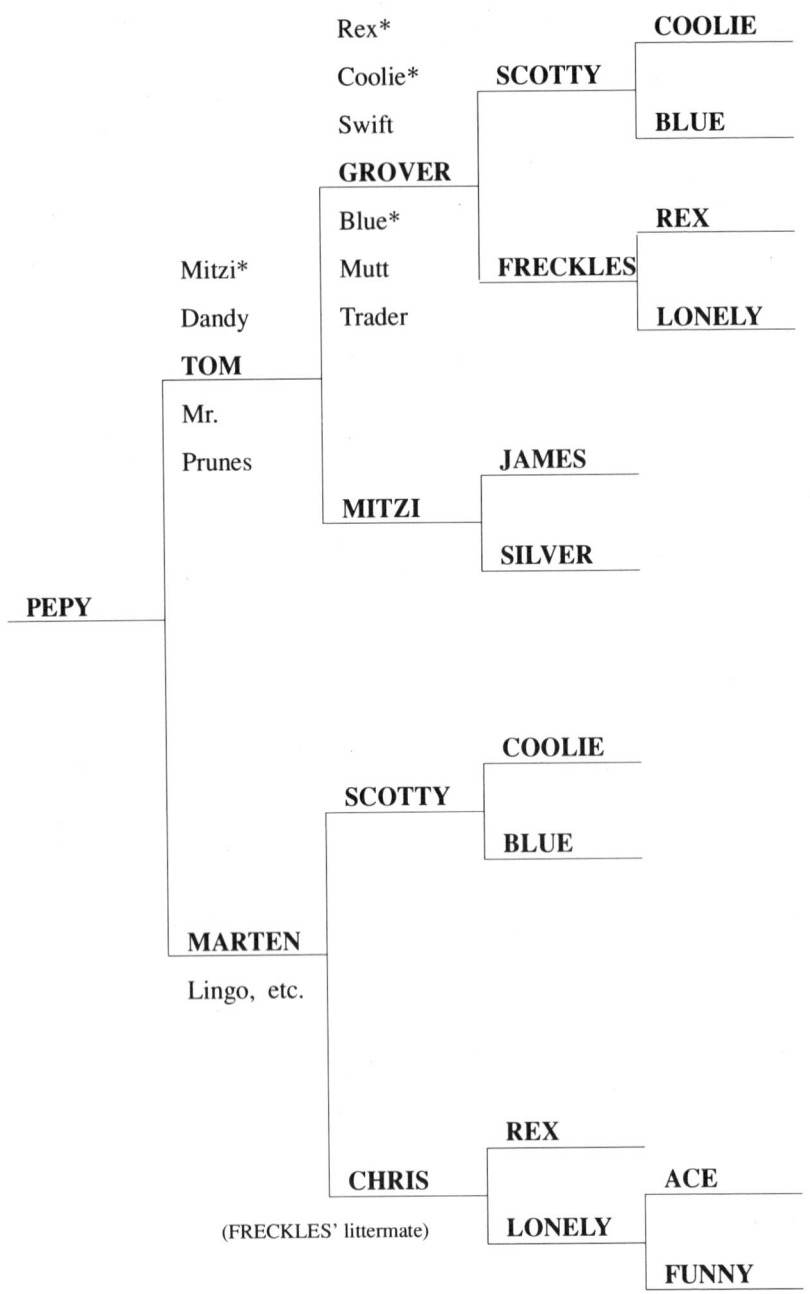

Building A Good Dog Team

First, several names appear more than once. The names with the asterisk after them are not the same dog as the dog with the same name without the asterisk. This simply illustrates George's predilection for using the same name over and over again (Gareth Wright is also notorious for this). It does make it confusing when you might find three different "Blue's" in his lot at the same time. Those dogs grouped in the vertical column are noteworthy littermates. The ones bred are shown in caps.

Pepy represented the perpetuation of George's line as he has developed it. Then George sold Pepy and went to Lingo as his main stud. Pictures of Scotty, Blue, James, and Coolie may all be found in George's book.

Let's take a brief look at each of the dogs shown in this pedigree starting from the oldest. Coolie, Blue, and Rex all represent the best of George's old guard and the village strains. Blue was mother to many top dogs. Rex was George's main stud before Scotty. He sent Rex to Huslia one summer after he had moved to Fairbanks to keep that blood in the village breeding.

Lonely was bred by Bill Taylor and owned by several people before George obtained her. Lonely was part Wright hound. She was out of a Wright hound named Ace (Gareth attributes the attitude in many later dogs to Ace) and one of the famous "German dogs" that Bill Taylor raced. Henry Reinhardt bred those dogs. One of them, named Funny, was Lonely's mother. George bred Lonely to Rex and produced a seminal litter that included the bitches responsible for George's success for many years (both from the performance of Freckles and the offspring of Freckles and Chris). The dogs in this Rex x Lonely litter were Freckles, Chris, Dot, Mopsie and one other that went back to the village that George said never turned out.

Of these dogs, Freckles was the most outstanding performer. She won the Rendezvous with George running next to Trot in double lead and the same year pulled George from behind to win the North American running the last five miles with two broken hands (Freckles, not George!).

Scotty was George's main stud for many years and an outstanding performer in his own right. He ran in eight North Americans for George, a feat that very few dogs will ever match. He was a leader who trained pups up until he was fifteen years old and finally died at the age of seventeen. Scotty was fairly heavy boned (although his offspring are not) and as the many pictures of him show, had the appearance of an archetypal husky. I had him at my yard for a few weeks several years ago to do some breeding. He was a very standoffish kind of dog, not shy, nor aggressive, but with a mind and presence all his own. In my mind, it was the equivalent of having Secretariat come stay at your house.

Though it was Freckles' first litter with Scotty that set the stage for what was to be a major trend in breeding, Chris will be known in this litter as the bitch whose pups were the most outstanding. George bred Scotty to both Freckles and Chris and several times stated that as impressed as he was with the Scotty x Freckles dogs, he thought Chris' pups were stronger. The first time one of the Scotty x Chris litters ever

"Lingo"
"... a Scotty x Chris pup that George described as his best ever."

Building A Good Dog Team

ran in harness, they ran the entire way of a seven mile trail. When George heard this he was so incredulous that he took them out himself the next day to see it with his own eyes, and they repeated their performance for him.

In analyzing the relations of these dogs, because Freckles and Chris are littermates, I am considering these pups out of Scotty to be more or less genetically identical (for the purpose of examining the pedigree). The importance of this will be seen when we look at Marten x Tom. The first Scotty x Freckles breeding produced Grover, Blue*, Coolie*, Swift (not the same Swift mentioned in George' book), Mutt, Trader, and Rex* (a dog that was sold as a pup to Peter Norberg and ran on Peter's winning North American team).

Every one of these pups made George's team. George attempted some very interesting breeding combinations with all these dogs, in-

"Scotty"
"Scotty" in his prime with "Jarvi" in lead during the 1970 North American. Scotty raced in eight North American Championships and was the foundation stud for George Attla's kennel. (Originally shown in *Everything I Know About Training & Racing Sled Dogs* by George Attla.)

cluding breeding Blue*, Coolie*, Mutt and Swift back to Huslia huskies (Swift was bred to a Bill Williams dog named Nellie. One of these pups ran on Peter Norberg's North American team-Nellie*). He also bred Trader back to Scotty. (The percentages of really fast dogs was not very high out of these breedings although one of the Scotty x Trader pups I am familiar with eventually threw several excellent dogs when outbred.)

By far the most successful combination of this litter occurred when Grover was bred to Mitzi. (Grover was eventually bought for breeding purposes by Chuck Gould in Minnesota, based in part on the very sound advice of Denis Christman, who stated that Grover represented untold years of the best breeding of Gareth Wright and George Attla, and the price was well worth it for the breeding alone.)

Mitzi is out of James and Silver. James was from George's old breed, a tough strong wheel dog that is pictured on page 224 of George's book. Silver was a female bred by Willie Keyse. Silver is behind many very fine dogs, especially in Gareth Wright's dog lot. When Mitzi was bred to Grover, another exceptional litter was produced that included Tom, Prunes, Mitzi*, Mr., and Dandy.

Prunes was the most outstanding performer of this litter. He lead George's team all three days of the 1980 North American at sixteen months of age. Dandy was sold to Sandy Saunderson in British Columbia as a pup and was the foundation stud for his and sons Rod and Ross' kennel, producing many fine dogs. Mitzi, Mr. and eventually, Prunes were all sold to Don Beland. George chose to breed Tom rather than Prunes because he preferred the finer boned build of Tom. Tom succeeded Scotty as main stud in the Attla lot.

Tom was bred to Marten. Marten is a Scotty x Chris pup and therefore pedigree-wise the same breeding as Tom's sire, Grover. Pepy was the outstanding get of the Tom x Marten breeding. Genetically speaking, Pepy's mother (Marten) is the same as his grandfather (Grover) on the father's side. This whole approach is striking a balance between keeping enough genetically similar material to perpetuate the integrity of the line, while not inbreeding so closely that the line deteriorates.

I have watched and followed these dogs and their whereabouts for several years. I grant you that it may be somewhat confusing after a quick reading of the connections, but this is a great example of excellent breeding that produced some excellent dogs. It is not necessarily a

Building A Good Dog Team

"cookbook", but an example of a lesson that can be taken from concrete success. I could just as easily have pointed to the successful breeding ventures of other well known mushers such as Gareth Wright, Harvey Drake, and Charlie Champaine. Each has taken a somewhat different approach with success.

One final note of significance to this breeding sequence; I mentioned earlier that these breedings set the stage for an entire trend that was replicated by many dog mushers. That is, George crossed the village husky to Gareth Wright's Aurora husky stock (as Gareth calls them, but most commonly known as Wright hounds). These breedings were not necessarily pure husky strain to pure Wright hound, but that combination began producing exceptional dogs. Harvey Drake used a Losonsky bred dog named Junior to cross with Wright hound type dogs to create his winning North American team and his leader, Demon, a big flop eared, blue eyed hound that breathed speed.

Joee Redington used a Junior x Queenie (Wright hound) pup named Gunner to sire hundreds of pups that rebuilt his team and kennel. The dogs Billy Barnes sold to Doug McRae that made up the bulk of his

"Demon"
Harvey Drake's leader, unbeatable in every way. The dog that "breathed speed."

winning 1984 North American team were Gunner offspring or descendants. Gunner's littermates, Nenana, Rowdy and Gusto also sired many excellent dogs. In recent years that the dogs which have combined the old village breed with the Wright hound strain have emerged dominant in many top racing kennels.

OTHER BREEDING PERMUTATIONS

There are some notable exceptions to be sure. Charlie Champaine's team was about as dominant a dog team could be in 1984 and he did not have this type of breeding in his team, although he had some pups of that ilk in his yard that suggested that might change. After he married Roxy Wright, two very strong lines were crossed that produced a dog team that George Attla described as the best he had ever raced against.

Charlie advises looking at the strong points not just in an individual dog, but in the close ancestors. If a dog is superior but has one area that is a weakness (poor feet, for example) she needs to be bred to a dog who not only has good feet, but whose immediate ancestors also strongly showed that trait. Ideally the progeny of that dog could also be examined. This is where the knowledge of other dog people can be especially helpful, people who knew the dogs behind the prospective stud.

If you are looking to breed in specific traits, don't try to obtain something shown further back than grandparents. The genetic effect further back than grandparents is very dilute and most difficult to isolate.

Stated obviously, building a good dog team requires having good dogs. This means a person needs to either buy or breed successfully to get those select dogs. Put another way, building a good dog team means avoiding bum dogs.

Denis Christman was a breeder who rarely had more than ten adult dogs in his yard. Yet he sold innumerable dogs that competed on the very best teams in the Rendezvous, the North American, the Iditarod and every other major race. He had a reputation for selling only very good dogs. If you got a dog from Denis Christman, you got a good dog. He was exacting in his judgement of young dogs. His standard, though I have never seen it written anywhere was very demanding. If the dog did not measure up to that standard he would not keep it. He did not hang on to question marks.

Building A Good Dog Team

Denis has said that it is necessary to sell some good dogs. If you hung on to every pup until you were absolutely positive that the dog was really good or just average, you would be inundated with bums. He felt it simply was not worth having all those questionable mouths around just to try to guarantee that an odd good dog slipped through the lot. And if a good dog does slip through the cracks, it will enhance the reputation of the breeder and should increase the salability of his dogs in the future.

It is a very difficult maxim for 99% of us to abide by: "never keep a bum." That doesn't mean that you have to eliminate every dog in your lot that does not meet your criteria for owning, but don't kid yourself, if a dog doesn't meet your standards, it will compromise them. A team

Denis Christman bred and contributed dogs to many championship teams. Denis always felt he was too big to race. He bred dogs, trained them and shared what he knew. He <u>was</u> a big man. *Photo by Lisa Fallgren Stevens.*

The Speed Mushing Manual

can go only as fast as the slowest dog. The standard of your kennel may be measured not by your best dog but by your worst.

It is not easy to produce a good dog, or to buy a good dog or to have the candor to get rid of a dog which is not up to standard. All three are essential, however, to building a good dog team.

Gareth Wright
Gareth Wright blasts out of the chute at the Tok Race of Champions. Leaders are Spot and Queenie. *Photo by Lisa Fallgren Stevens*

Chapter 3
Feed 'Em Good...

After winning a race in Anchorage, Gareth Wright was asked by a newspaper reporter how he made his dogs run so fast. Gareth responded in the most capsulated form, "You've got to feed 'em good and treat 'em right." Racing dogs today are athletes and must be fueled and conditioned as such.

It is no longer sufficient to throw them a dried fish or give them a bowl of grocery store crunchies if they are to perform competitively. At the peak of performance, a dog's body and mind are finely tuned. A dog driver knows this and must build and protect this physical and mental conditioning that is maintained in such delicate balance.

Some of the simplest and most easily controlled factors relevant to performance are frequently overlooked. Of these, the feed a dog is given is probably the most outstanding. It is puzzling that people can realize the desirability of having good dogs, go to tremendous effort, time and expense to get good dogs and yet virtually ignore the importance of their diets to their performance.

If you want a pet, feed it like a pet. If you want a racing sled dog, feed it like the athlete it is. Even an unseasoned eye will see results produced by a really excellent diet. How dogs act, how they look, how their muscles feel, are all dramatically affected by diet. The effects will not be seen overnight, as these are long term and long lasting effects. Still, after a month you should begin to notice some changes. Coats will be shinier, the dogs will be more active and exuberant. Muscles will be harder, especially the back of the thighs and those running along the back.

The quality of the diet of a sled dog will also have less visible, but critically important results relative to the general health of a dog, the soundness of his structure and the condition of the running machinery. We know this is true because of the controlled research and documentation that has been conducted in the last fifteen years, and from the proof of performance, the diets of the winning teams.

Over the last fifteen years, considerable attention has been paid to developing the very best diet for racing dogs as mushers sought a competitive edge and a means to maximize the potential of their dogs.

Dr. David Kronfeld devoted considerable attention in his collaboration with musher Harris Dunlap on the subject of optimal nutritional formulas for racing dogs. Dunlap himself was a proponent of a "zero carbohydrate" diet for a time, (this position was later modified) and became associated with an idea totally in contrast to what all the commercial literature previously pontificated about canine dietary needs.

Even now, when most competitive mushers will testify to the importance of a predominantly meat diet, there remains much popular literature and commercial interests which support the idea that dogs should be fed primarily grains and cereals. The performance results should settle any debate, but Kronfeld and Dunlap's legitimate efforts have certainly brought some scientific credence to the normal ballyhoo surrounding nutritional issues for dogs. Although I am fairly certain that neither of these men would claim that their findings are the last word on nutritional needs of race dogs, they have thrown some valuable information into the "food bucket." The fact that an attempt was made to take a controlled and objective look at nutritional requirements and benefits for racing sled dogs is in itself significant.

Kronfeld and Dunlap's publications emphasize a different vocabulary of nutrition that opens the door for further objective study, but the performance diets used by top dog drivers today will still command the most deserved attention.

I doubt if any dog musher will ever accept the concept of the perfect diet (unless perhaps it is their own). No matter how well formulated, no matter how well proven, he will always modify it seeking something just a little bit better. The summer after he won the World Championship in Anchorage, Charlie Champaine passed out flyers at a State Fair explaining exactly how and what he fed his dogs. I doubt if more than a few will precisely replicate his feeding program despite the proven success.

Feed 'Em Good

The relationship of stress to dietary needs is important to race dogs. Kronfeld repeatedly emphasizes this factor. The work and pressure on a racing sled dog has implications far beyond the need for increased calories. He estimates that at least 30% of the caloric needs (metabolizable energy) of a dog should be supplied by protein in order to maintain red blood cell levels. This is especially important to the oxygen carrying capacity of a dog. Not more than 15% should be carbohydrate (again this is metabolizable energy, not the percentages that you read on a label) and that fat should be the primary source of energy for the well fueled sled dog.

The source of this energy should be meat. That is more than my bias. Every study that Kronfeld and Dunlap did and the performance of every winning dog team in Alaska points to the same conclusion. If you are not feeding meat, forget all the old wives tales, and do it. Chicken, beef, horse, are all fine dog feed. Dunlap talks of his feed at this writing consisting of chicken, pork lungs, and rice.

I have been feeding chicken, horse, beef, eggs, liver, corn oil, bone meal and enough commercial food (maybe 15%) to give form to a dog's stool. Charlie Champaine's feed is very similar although he doesn't use horse. Seal, beaver, and lamb are also very commonly used in Alaska. Once you have fed meat for any length of time, I doubt you will ever revert to cereals as the dietary mainstay. The benefits are that obvious.

Tremendous advances have been made in the last ten years in the quality of dry commercial food available. The top quality foods are much closer than ever before to a quality meat based diet. The idea of a dry food being the best you can feed is an appealing one. I remain skeptical that a dehydrated, processed food by itself can ever match the quality of a fresh or frozen meat based diet. I would certainly welcome such an achievement. The best of the premium commercial dry foods are getting closer, but it hasn't happened yet.

Dogs who are fed meat are stronger and more active. They start the season physically tougher and have tougher attitudes. They will muscle up faster when young and toughen in faster as adults. It makes them obnoxious in summer if you don't exercise them. They are more active, dig holes, break chains, tear houses apart and leap tall buildings in a single bound. They will also start their fall conditioning program looking like they already have two hundred miles on them.

Both research and performance have yielded so much more advanced information than was available even ten years ago. If you look at any dog team finishing in the top ten of the Rendezvous or the North American, you should note that without exception, every team was fed a primarily meat diet. It is only astonishing that people who know this fail to draw the obvious conclusion.

For years, it seemed that commercial dog food makers were stressing that you would starve your dog if fed nothing but (muscle) meat. Even then, people knew that a critical element in any diet was the balance of nutrients, but what was not clearly understood, was the optimal elements in the diet of a dog under stress. Kronfeld's studies and the results achieved by winning dog drivers have more accurately defined what a proper balance of nutrients is for a racing sled dog.

DIETARY BALANCE

Certainly dogs must have sources of vitamins, minerals and all the other elements of a sound diet. There are sources of these elements now used by almost every competitive musher I know, however, that are still ignored by people who have not experienced the benefits of feeding meat as the largest portion of their dogs' diet. After the years of propaganda saturation about the lurking evils of meat diets, it is understandable that most people are hesitant to jump into something which does not have the official sanction of a brand name dog food company. A balanced diet IS essential, but I am not convinced the optimal mix for a race dog yet comes out of a dog food bag.

PREPARATION OF FOODS

Until I am convinced otherwise, I believe meat should be used as the basis of a diet not as a supplementary component. The rice or a small amount of commercial food added for fiber and carbohydrates is the supplement in a meat based diet that has been fueling all the winning teams for many, many years.

Non game meat such as chicken, beef, horse and liver should not be cooked. Cooking needlessly destroys too many good things. Moose, caribou, and other wild ungulates need to be cooked to avoid tapeworm problems. Seal, pork and bear all present the possibility of trichinosis. The incidence is very low in seal and pork. In the fur seal which is available in Alaska, less than one percent of the seals carry trichinosis.

Freezing meat at very cold temperatures (-20F) for at least a month is said to further lessen the potential for your dog getting trichinosis.

Feed 'Em Good

The choice is yours. There is a slight risk, but trichinosis is a very serious problem for any dog that gets it, very possibly the end of that dogs running career.

Beaver is fed both ways. Iditarod racers generally feed it bones and all and I have never heard of a problem resulting from that, although every driver I know who is competing in speed races does not feed the beaver bones. It is a very laborious process to bone out a beaver, especially if it hasn't been cooked. Still, whether there is sufficient cause for concern or not, everyone I know takes the time to bone them.

Beaver is pretty amazing stuff. On the Iditarod, where keeping dogs eating is often a major difficulty, beaver is one of the last things dogs will refuse to eat. Dogs love it (Beef by-products are another palate pleaser). It will put weight on your dogs very quickly and has a very sturdy reputation for making dogs strong. Beaver is available from Minnesota fur farms or as a by product of trappers' catch.

Fish (mostly chum salmon and whitefish) are still fed quite a bit in the summer time, but most competitive drivers will concur that fish does not compare favorably to meat as a staple for a race team. I fed my team fish for a year. I replaced half of the commercial food I was feeding at the time with fish. I allowed one salmon for every eight dogs. The results were far superior to the straight commercial food, but could not compare with the meat based diet I now use. Still, fish has some very positive things going for it and should not be ruled out altogether.

Salmon needs to be cooked if it was simply split and dried (as mine was) in order to kill parasites as well as to rehydrate it. Otherwise the parasites in salmon seem very easily dispatched by hard freezing as described above. Most people I know still cook it, nonetheless.

While some people like to soak their food so that it becomes a paste, I simply put all the ingredients in a bucket, add hot water and mix it up. I use a shoulder length rubber "trapper's glove" to mix it thoroughly into a delectably dripping mud consistency.

DIETARY SUPPLEMENTS

There are some other good feed items that can add in to a good diet. Eggs are 100% useable by a dog. They are high in protein and surprisingly, have a fair amount of fat as well. Corn oil is used as a fat source by many mushers I know and contains other valuable nutrients (e.g., Vitamin E). Easily digested, it is said to be a complete fat for dogs.

Lard and tallow are also commonly used as a fat supplement. Though lard is usually much more expensive, it is far superior to tallow. In fact, I would not recommend tallow under any circumstances. There are too many other things available that are far better.

A cup or two of bone meal in the food bucket and a couple ounces of liver for each dog will insure the adequate presence of vitamins, calcium and other micronutrients and trace elements we assume a dog needs. Many people also add wheat germ oil, B vitamins or one of the "blood building concoctions" such as "Red Cell," or "V.A.L. Syrup" which is high in B vitamins, iron and other elements related to production of red blood cells.

The value of these and other additives is always debatable, though each has its ardent supporters. Many people use them with the idea that, "it probably won't hurt, and if there is a possibility that it will help, it is worth the money."

Vitamins, especially B12, B6, B15 and C have always provided great allure to athletes, although the fascination has always been more notable than any documented benefit. At least it provides material for debate and opinion after the races when the winning combination is usually dissected in an attempt to find the secret combination.

There is some suggestion that Vitamin C is a useful supplement for dogs under racing stress. Kronfeld and Dunlap have done some small scale comparisons of dogs under stress given Vitamin C supplement versus dogs who have been given no Vitamin C supplementation. Kronfeld felt the blood indices significant enough to recommend giving 50 to 200 mg. per day to each dog under stress. Larry Tallman told me that he believes Vitamin C helps his dogs resist sickness and recover faster than dogs who don't get a Vitamin C supplement.

WATER

The most critically important dietary element is water. It is frequently overlooked or paid too little attention. It is the cheapest, yet most important nutrient that a dog will consume.

Doc Lombard laughed when he recalled on some of his early trips to Alaska that he felt enlightened because he provided his dogs with a shovelful of fresh snow to eat whereas most of the other dogs he observed were expected to eat whatever snow was available to get their water. Today every racer knows how important hydration is to a race dog and takes great pains to make sure the dogs drink.

Feed 'Em Good

When you watch marathon runners take water several times during the course of a race, you can get some hint of the importance of hydration and the role water plays in muscle metabolism. Dehydration will knock a dog down very quickly, and he will not be able to perform well until he is completely rehydrated.

In summertime, I like to have water available all the time to a dog, either through a full cool can or bowl or if you prefer, an "on-demand" watering device such as Doc Lombard uses. In winter and when the dog is exercising strenuously, careful attention must be given to monitor the water intake of each dog. Since water will freeze if not drunk immediately, the dog must usually be encouraged to drink as soon as water is placed before him. This is easily accomplished by flavoring the water.

I have used liver or beaver drippings, corn oil, canned dog food, electrolyte powder, and a few other items to tempt the water palate of

"water...is the cheapest but most important nutrient that a dog will consume." *Photo by Lisa Fallgren Stevens*

my dogs. What has worked out easiest, cheapest, and most successful is to pour warm water into my food bucket which has a little bit of food from the previous feeding left over, stir it up and deliver to my slavering pooches. For the morning watering I have a chunk of Beef By products in the water. Dogs love this broth and it provides the necessary amounts of iodine that might be otherwise hard to find.

My dogs get at least a quart of water in the morning and another in the afternoon or evening in addition to that which is mixed with their food. The morning of a race I give them their morning quart of water about three hours prior to their starting time. This schedule came about from a trial and error approach as well as observing patterns of other winning drivers.

My regimen seems to keep the dogs well hydrated under ordinary circumstances, but after a particularly grueling race like the Rendez-vous, I feel it is more effective to deliver several smaller water portions over a period of hours so that absorption is enhanced. The human stomach is only able to absorb about 26 ounces of water per hour, though I do not know what the water absorption capacity of a dog is. Instead of my normal two waterings, I would have three or four.

DEHYDRATION

If you are in a position to weigh your dogs between heats, every pound lost should be compensated for by 16 ounces of water. A dog has to have those fluids replaced. If not he will be better off staying home the next day. You can check for gross dehydration by lifting the skin of the dog's back and observing the resilience by which it returns to its normal position (Do this when you know the dog is normal to develop an idea of what should happen). If it returns to its former position like molasses in January, you have some serious hydrating to accomplish and a very doubtful starter for tomorrow.

Electrolyte solutions have been more commonly used in recent years. The idea is to restore the fluid levels in the body faster and to replace the key elements within those fluids so that metabolism can proceed normally. Water is the key and there is very little supporting evidence for any significant benefit to a animal that is not severely depressed.

If you do use these powders, use them the night before, not the morning of the race. Though this was apparently common knowledge to other people who were using these solutions, I learned this lesson the

Feed 'Em Good

hard way, watching my young swing dog vomit her way through the third day of the Rendezvous. That was a mighty tough minded dog.

Human runners now very commonly consume up to sixteen ounces of water within the half hour before their event. Only in recent years have we seen this done at the race track. Several people initially tried giving a cup or two of water to a dog ten or fifteen minutes before the race to prevent a particular dog from dipping snow. Now we see it more frequently with hydration as the motive, although it is far from common practice.

Water intake should be increased if feed is increased. As you get into heavier training and the dogs start eating more, make sure they get an equivalent increase in the amount of water in their bowl. Bigger dogs will take a little more water than smaller dogs. If your dogs are reluctant drinkers, try watering them about two hours after feeding. I am told that this is the is the time of greatest metabolic demand for water. I don't know if that is true, but I do know that dogs will consume water more readily at this interval.

A well designed meat diet has several other advantages beyond those already described. The amount of manure you will have to shovel will drop dramatically. Meat is a more efficient food, hence less waste produced. And if you look around a little, you will probably find that your total food cost is very comparable to what you might otherwise be feeding.

If your dogs have shown the anal capillary bleeding during hard running, you will probably find this will disappear once the dogs have been on a meat diet for awhile.

Dogs fed a diet consisting primarily of meat will far outperform equivalent dogs fed a commercial diet. It won't make great dogs out of mediocre ones, but it will make a good dog better. If you want to build your dogs up you need a diet that will provide the building blocks to allow the dog to develop his fitness potential. There will be skeptics who won't feed meat for one reason or another, but as one champion has said, "those aren't the guys who are going to call 'trail' on you."

I don't believe that there is a single "optimal diet" for race dogs but there are many performance proven formulas that might be a good place to start - and finish. My own diet is very similar to Charlie Champaine's though not exactly the same, especially in proportions.

I use horse rather than beef but if I had to choose just one meat, I would select chicken. I generally feed less oil because I live in a warmer climate than Charlie. I adjust the corn oil levels as the winter temperature changes, adding more when it is colder, less when it warms up.

A meat based diet does need to be carefully formulated to insure a proper balance and the inclusion of necessary nutrients. Here is the formula that Charlie Champaine passed out the summer following his World Championship in 1984.

CHARLIE'S RACE DIET

For 24 dogs:

Beef	30%
Chicken	30%
Egg	5%
Liver	20%
2 cup bone meal	
1 cup wheat germ oil	
2 cup corn oil	
1 cup Red Cell	
dry commercial feed	15%

Start using liver September 1st. Use small quantities at first and work up to 20% by mid-November. Start feeding race diet September 1st.

SUMMER DIET

Beef	60%
Chicken	20%
Egg	5%
dry commercial feed	15%
2 cup bone meal	
1 cup wheat germ oil	

Chapter Four
Elements of Conditioning

"There ain't no substitute for tough." "Tough" means a dog has the physical conditioning on him to make him go easily and go far. Proper conditioning requires a step by step process. There is no way around it, no shortcuts, and no easy ways out. Conditioning must be approached deliberately and diligently in order to produce a team which is physically fit and mentally strong.

The words, "conditioning" and "training" are often used interchangeably. I try to use the word "conditioning" to mean the physical and athletic building of the body and "training" to mean teaching a dog to do something. Nonetheless, I am often guilty myself of talking about "fall training" when really I mean "fall conditioning."

Both conditioning and training utilize many of the same procedures. As dogs are conditioned they also acquire a great deal of training. No athlete can reach his potential and no dog team can be seriously competitive without benefit of an extensive and carefully planned conditioning program. Though in practice, most conditioning and training transpire during the same period of involvement with the dogs, I will try to talk primarily about "conditioning" in this chapter.

A driver wants speed, response, smoothness, attitude and several hundred other attributes for his team, none of which is so basic as physical conditioning and none which can be so easily affected by the driver as the condition of his team.

What peak physical condition means for any athlete depends on the kind of activity engaged in. The most important elements of physical fitness for a racing sled dog are strength, endurance (muscular and cardio vascular), speed, agility, balance, and neuromuscular coordination. Each of these aspects must be addressed in an informed and well planned conditioning program for optimal results.

STRENGTH

Once the sled is moving fast enough to be "on step" (much like a boat or plane) the amount of resistance an individual dog has to overcome is relatively small. Nonetheless, a sled dog is a pulling animal. The structure is designed to pull and his musculature developed accordingly. When going through fresh or deep snow, sprinting up a steep hill, or running in a relatively small team, strength is an asset to the dog and to the team.

Most of us would prefer a bigger, stronger dog if we were convinced that it had the same speed and endurance of a smaller dog. Because a few strong dogs can pull as much as several weaker dogs, its strength and pulling power could make for a better team. However, speed and endurance are more critical than sheer brute strength.

Perhaps of greater importance than the absolute pulling power that strengthening exercise gives, is the protection to the critical joints primarily engaged in running. Injuries to the front shoulder are among the most common and the most dreaded for a racing sled dog, especially if it is to the joint itself rather than a muscle in the same area.

Unless very careful treatment and therapy are conducted, these kind of injuries can be recurrent and ultimately chronic. Strengthening exercises build and firm the muscles surrounding the joints, increasing stability, cushioning the joint from impact and force contrary to the intended range of motion of that joint.

Strength is generally addressed in early season conditioning, when muscles are soft and dogs want to run with reckless abandon. Look for strength to develop from cart training, running in small teams, and hill work. We don't need or want incredible hulks of dogs. We want well muscled dogs with firm and safe joint protection.

ENDURANCE

If you have ever run yourself, you may have experienced two very different factors that limit your endurance. The first is experienced as running out of breath, being winded or just plain pooping out. This is a limitation of cardio vascular (aerobic) endurance.

The second, muscular endurance, is the ability to sustain a sub-maximal muscular effort for an extended period of time. At the end stage of muscular endurance capability, the muscle fatigue is akin to throwing peanut butter inside a mechanical engine, everything just comes to a slow motion kind of halt, where the spirit may be willing but the flesh cannot meet the task.

When building up muscular endurance, the day following a heavy workout will undoubtedly be marked by sore muscles and a feeling of heaviness in the legs. This comes from the breaking down or micro tearing of muscles tissue and from the depletion of glycogen stores in the muscles. Both of these processes are normal. The muscles tissue will grow back stronger and the glycogen will soon be restored, given adequate nutrients and time.

Much research has been done on cardio vascular (aerobic) endurance and to a lesser degree, muscular endurance, on human athletes. Cardio vascular (aerobic) fitness is measured by maximum oxygen uptake and muscular endurance is measured by the velocity at which lactate begins to add up and seep into the bloodstream, or the "velocity before onset of blood lactate accumulation" (VOBLA).

Both of these measurements indicate aspects of endurance that are important to a well conditioned sled dog. The ability to get as much oxygen to the muscles as possible through a high oxygen uptake and carrying capacity of the blood allows a continuous expenditure of a very high level of exertion without dumping inhibiting levels of lactate into the bloodstream.

Lactate (lactic acid) is a chemical produced when exercising muscles require more oxygen that can be supplied through the cardio vascular system. Muscles can only tolerate a small amount of lactate before it starts shutting down the functioning of the muscle. It feels as if the muscles are grinding to a burning halt. This is the limitation of a dead out sprint and why pacing is so critical in anything more than a very short distance.

The ability to tolerate lactate buildup is a quality which can very much be extended through proper conditioning, but many athletes, canine and human, are genetically endowed with a greater lactate tolerance capacity from the very start.

Championship dog teams are often impressive because of their strong finishing. The trait of "coming home hard" is a pacing strategy that is trained into the best dog teams. It has its basis in what is the most athletically and physiologically efficient way to run a given distance fastest.

If you observe running and swimming races you will notice that over the last fifteen years or so, a pacing strategy has developed to prevent lactate buildup. The method is sometimes known as "negative splits." Instead of starting out hard and trying to maintain, the racer runs or swims each lap faster than the one before. In this manner, he or she is always working within his or her aerobic limits. As the body warms up, the pace is gradually speeded up. This approach has resulted in many a world record.

SPEED

Some dogs are simply born faster than others. The slowest greyhound is always going to be faster than the fastest Malemute. But an individual dog can only reach its full speed potential through optimal conditioning. A dog does not come off the stake with an ability to run as fast as his ultimate potential, not for very far anyway, without a rigorous conditioning program.

In the early portion of a conditioning program, the same exercises that help build strength will also help speed, since speed is dependent on strength and power among other factors. When hill training is discussed later, bear in mind the seeming paradox that slow heavy work can contribute positively to speed. This does not mean that you keep your dogs running slowly all the time pulling massive loads up tall mountains. It means that there is a very beneficial time and place for slow, hard pulling. Research from nearly every sport shows that slow, high intensity strength work improves speed.

Speed for a dog team really has two practical meanings, the basic pace that a team will travel with no special commands or pressure from the driver, and the top end, the highest sprint speed that a dog is capable of running for a relatively short distance. The basic pace is something which is established during the conditioning and training process, primarily through structuring the conditioning situations so that the dogs develop a habit of traveling at the desired basic pace.

Top end speed is primarily determined by genetics, and developed to full potential during the conditioning phase. Getting the dogs to run at top speed in races is a function of training, which will be more specifically addressed in a later chapter. Though conditioning and training must be understood as equally crucial elements for a top

Elements of Conditioning

performing dog team, they are often conducted at the same time and in the same context.

BALANCE, AGILITY & NEUROMUSCULAR COORDINATION

All of these factors are best attended to through repetition of the specific skill that an athlete will use in competition, namely, running in harness in the team. Balance and agility are both critical factors for a sled dog. As a remember of a multi member unit, connected by a series of taut lines, a dog does not always have a great latitude of choice as to where he is going and what obstacles he can avoid. At high speed, a very small clump or patch of ice in the trail can cause a slip or stumble sufficient to injure a muscle, joint, or tendon.

The ability to maintain balance and avoid these micro obstacles will perhaps not pay off right away, but in the long run it is your best protection against injury and the disappointment of putting so much into a dog only to see him not able to participate because of injury.

Neuromuscular coordination is the ability to make muscles do what the brain is trying to tell them to do. Motor planning and neurological pathways are developed and enhanced best by practice specific to the athletic task at hand. Dogs are creatures of habit. So are muscles. If you will be racing on hills, you need to do at least some training on hills. If you are racing on flat lightning fast trails you need to do some conditioning on lightning fast trails.

The development of neuromuscular coordination is as close an analogy to the training process as I can think of. By putting the body through a repetition of correctly performed tasks, the neuro motor pathways are improved so that performance can be achieved faster, more efficiently and more reliably.

And although slow heavy pulling is very beneficial at times, an appreciation of the need for neuromuscular coordination helps explain why it is unwise to always run with weight in the sled or a (heaven forbid) tire dragging behind the sled. Tire dragging is another subject that I will discuss the foibles of later.

SUMMARY

These are the key elements that make up fitness and conditioning for a race dog. The best manner to approach peak levels of condition is

The Speed Mushing Manual

Balance, Agility, and Neuromuscular Coordination - "at high speed, a very small clump or patch of ice in the trail can cause a slip or stumble sufficient to injure..." Note the dog with tail up anticipating the patch of ice ahead. *Photo by Lisa Fallgren Stevens*

Elements of Conditioning

subject to much opinion and debate. A large body of research exists on conditioning for human athletes as well as laboratory animals such as rats. Though many of these studies have questionable application to dogs, some general approaches and principles have proven valid and worthwhile to many mushers when applied to race dogs.

We thus rely on the utilization of the best and seemingly most relevant information available from human athlete research and the large body of knowledge derived from practical application by dog drivers who have demonstrated an ability to produce performance results.

Most dog teams in most races are under conditioned. A team of good dogs that are well fed, well cared for and well conditioned will surpass the performance of the vast majority of teams in most races. This is a very simple competitive advantage that most people choose to ignore, seeking magical explanations or formulas to make their team more competitive, when they were simply beaten by someone who put more time and effort into his team.

There is no substitute for tough. When the chips are down, it is the physically tough team that will shine. A tough team is capable of doing more things more easily. As the grind and pressure of training and racing wear on through the season, the team can more easily handle it because it has so much more reserve than the team which is always forced to operate at the brink of its current capacity.

The tough team can operate at 80% and still out perform a similar team performing at 100% of capacity that was not conditioned as well. A tough dog team is one that has been trained well, has a naturally instilled and nurtured sense of motivation and is very, very physically fit for the kind of tasks it will be performing. There are no substitutes, especially at the finish line.

"Doc"
Roland "Doc" Lombard, a true champion. *Photo by Paul McCormick*

Chapter Five
Elements of Training

"... the dog never makes a mistake. He is just a dog and he does what he does because he is a dog and thinks like a dog. It is you that makes the mistake because you haven't trained him to do want you want him to do when you want him to do it. Or you have misjudged what he is able to do, physically or mentally. So if a mistake is made in the team, it is you that has made it, not the dog."

- George Attla
Everything I Know About Training and Racing Sled Dogs

A good dog driver understands how to condition dogs. A better dog driver also understands how to train dogs. When all the dogs are selected and cared for, fed and conditioned, it is the training which distinguishes one dog team (and musher) from the rest. Training is what makes a dog team great and a ride that is worth it all.

It is commonly believed that the best dog team wins the race. And though this is usually true, it is also true that less gifted dog teams have often won big races because of the training ability of the driver. George Attla once told me that if winning was just a matter of who had the fastest dogs, it wouldn't be any fun. Later in the same conversation he said, "training dogs is the easiest thing in the world." I remember at the time merely staring at him blankly trying to think how I could get an explanation that would make it seem that easy to me.

Training is everything you do with your dogs and everything they go through. From the most trivial of interactions with your dogs to their hardest conditioning and running, every contact you have with your dogs and every experience they have can either help or hinder the effort to mold a top performing team.

I acquired a dog that had been raised by Carl Huntington. Carl's kids played with her as a pup and taught her various tricks. Every time she got the trick right they clapped and cheered and made a big happy fuss over her. When this dog grew up to be a Rendezvous leader, she loved the crowds. She loved the clapping and cheering and acted like it was all just for her. The tremendous din of Fourth Avenue has put more than one dog over the edge. But for this dog, it was as if she was a puppy again, right at home. More than any dog I have watched, this dog actually seemed to enjoy the bedlam of Fourth Avenue and always responded with a burst of speed. You might say those kids gave her Rendezvous training.

Most mushers I know started by observing others and imitating the procedures of an established musher. That is, if they were fortunate they had the opportunity to watch a good dog driver. Many were probably able to learn fundamental procedures without ever having had to learn how to articulate why they were doing what they were doing.

Some of the great dog drivers from the Alaskan villages may be unable to explain why they do something or tell you why it works, but they are masters of training. They learned from observation and generations of experience. They will tell you, "I don't know if this is the best way, but it is the way I do it."

Whether you learned how to train dogs by watching your father train dogs as many Alaskan mushers like Roxy Wright, Marvin Kokrine, Curtis and Chuck Erhart have, or learned from trial and error, reading all the books and gathering information and advice from whatever source is available, a good dog musher still has to put it all together. He must understand the whole picture in order to deal with unique situations and individual differences. The vocabulary and the jargon may be different, but the principles are the same and dogs are still trained the same way.

Training dogs is nothing more than teaching dogs to do what you want them to do, when you want them to do it. It requires an understanding of how dogs learn, experience, good judgement and a certain sense that makes a person "doggy." No book can adequately prepare a trainer, for although a certain amount of knowledge can be acquired from reading, it has to be honed by experience and application. The only

Elements of Training

way I know is to fill up your brain and roll up your sleeves. There is a science to it, but the best trainers are artists, truly.

There are some basic principles of training and learning that every dog musher should understand. Every good dog musher does.

A dog lot will gradually come to express each driver's personal preference and bias for the type of dog he prefers, and the kind of dog that will respond best to him. Some prefer big dogs, some prefer smaller dogs. Some prefer the screaming, foaming, bleeding from the ears to go blasters, some want a more reserved dog that will respond to training more reliably. Each type of dog and driver will do better with different emphasis on the type and tone of training utilized. A dog team requires a dog trainer who knows what applies best to each dog and how and when to apply it.

Chuck Erhart

Curtis Erhart

Photos by Paul McCormick

I heard one highly respected driver once state that "Alaskans like the kind of dog they can beat on." Though this is certainly a sweeping generalization, I think it would be fair to say that the good Alaskan drivers don't like to beat on dogs but do appreciate dogs that would be capable of standing up to that kind of treatment simply because of what that says about a dog's mental makeup. Those are the dogs that are not likely to quit or bolt or fold under the intense race pressure that top teams face. Those are tough minded dogs.

As different breeds of dogs have been added to the racing husky strains, many very fast dogs with much weaker minds have been produced. Though everyone I know wants a physically talented athlete, the most important part of the dog is still between the ears. When a race gets really tough and a dog team is working at the edge of its physical limits, the tough minded dogs are found in front, not lying down wrapped around a tree.

A TRAINING OUTLINE

My approach to training relies on three steps:

1. Setting up the situation so the dogs will do what you want as a function of the situation and the dogs natural inclinations. This establishes correct habits.
2. Pairing anticipated behaviors with verbal cues and reinforcing correct responses. This teaches dogs the meaning of your select verbal cues.
3. Translating a cue into a command by insisting the appropriate response be executed. This insures that the dogs do what the driver wants, when he wants it done.

STEP # 1

Set up the training situation so the dogs will perform correctly. This requires planning and preparation. Your job is to set up the situation so that the dogs cannot fail.

As an example, suppose you have some young dogs that have never passed before and you suspect there might be trouble. To avoid this you must decide how to set up the situation so they will succeed. In that way you will have success to expand upon, not problems to correct.

Elements of Training

You do this by making success as easy as possible. Maybe you will set up the first situation so as to have one person and one dog parked well off the trail when you go by. The team goes by easily. "Atta boy!"

The next time you make the situation a little more challenging so the success will ingrain the correct habit a little deeper. You might bring another team closer to the trail but still off it. Success again, and so on, each time making the situation closer to what the dog will later encounter. Each time the dog successfully negotiates these progressively staged situations, the right habit is strengthened.

STEP # 2

Attach a verbal cue to a desired behavior. As you get to know what the dogs can and will do in different circumstances, give a verbal cue just before a desired behavior is about to happen.

When we train sled dogs we start with dogs that have been bred for a function. Any dog that has been bred for a function has natural inclinations that make the job of a trainer easier.

For example, if your dogs are in harness tied to the hook up post, screaming to go, it is a fair assumption that when you pull the hook or snub line and give them a cue ("Get Up," "O.K.," "Awright," "Hike," etc.) they will take off. It is situation where you can easily establish the association between the verbal cue and the desired response, i.e., to move forward. Every time the cue is given and the desired response follows, you are building and strengthening a connection in the dogs mind and teaching them the meaning of your cue.

Once this association is established, you can begin to shape this association so that you can elicit the desired response under a wider variety of circumstances. At first you can suggest the response under slightly more difficult circumstances. You can continue to build on the success of each increasingly difficult set of conditions as the dogs response reliability grows.

You set up the situation for the dogs to succeed, pair it with a cue and reinforce the correct response. If the dog was naturally inclined to execute the desired behavior, just allowing him to satisfy an innate drive can be reinforcing. A behavior that results in the dog getting what he wants is self reinforcing.

Each situation will probably suggest the most appropriate kind of reinforcement. You can do reinforce verbally ("Attaboy," "Good Dog," etc.) if your words are meaningful to your dogs. You can pat the dog up. You can throw him a tidbit back at the truck. Know what is positive to your dogs.

Remember to strengthen the meaning of your verbal reinforcers when you have the opportunity by connecting them to the good things in a dog's life, like when he's fed or when he gets petted. Make your verbal strokes meaningful to the dog.

STEP # 3

When the dog will perform on command even though he would prefer not to, he is trained. Once a dog knows the meaning of a verbal cue, and is capable of responding in the way you have defined, it is fair to insist on the correct response. I call this "trained insistence" and discuss it further in the next chapter. This means that a certain predefined response is not only probable following a given cue, but is required.

You will now control the probability so the correct response is delivered every time a command is given, because the dog was so trained and because you have insisted.

CUES AND COMMANDS

I make a distinction between the words "cue" and "command." A CUE is a signal or a prompt that is likely to elicit a specific response from a dog. This can be environmental or auditory, for example. A CUE is a signal to a dog that now is the time for something to happen. There is no force or enforcement involved in this. Usually it involves having built an association between a CUE and the desired response. The vast majority of dog training falls under this category.

A COMMAND is more than a request or a suggestion. It is a requirement, a demand, an insistence that when you give the COMMAND the dog responds in the way that you have defined. It means the dog should perform not only when he feels like it but every time you tell him to.

TRAINED TO DO WHAT?

Before any training begins you have to know what you are expecting and exactly what you are trying to train your dog to do. You must have a clear definition of terms and expectations in your own mind in

Elements of Training

order to communicate that to a dog. You cannot expect a dog to do something if you cannot clearly define what you want it to do.

Most of the questions related to training dogs lead to, "How can I make my dogs go faster?" But before that question can appropriately be asked, the more fundamental question needs to be answered, "What exactly do you want your dog to do?" What does "go faster" mean in concrete terms? If you want your dog to go faster when you say, "Get Up !," you have to define what is a satisfactory response.

When you say, "Get Up !" does that mean that the dog should be clawing at the earth with every ounce of energy? Does it mean that you have to feel a noticeable jerk on the gangline? Does it mean that you should see a tightening of the tugline? Does it mean that you should perceive the dog is trying harder? Does it mean that the dog is merely not holding back?

All of this has to be very specifically defined in terms clear enough so that you can also define your reactions in advance. Because equally important as defining what you want the dog to do, you have to clearly predefine how you will respond to every possible contingency that follows your COMMAND.

You tell a dog to "Get Up !" and it lies down. What do you do?

You tell a dog to "Get Up !" and he turns around and looks at you. What do you do?

You tell a dog to "Get Up !" and he claws and scratches with everything he's got but the rest of the team is merely sauntering along. What do you do?

Unfortunately, most people don't think of these things until they have already happened. The value of experience hopefully is that the next time that person will know in advance what he will do and can act confidently. It is fundamentally important that you know in advance exactly what you will do in any event, in any contingency. Predefining your response allows for training consistency. Consistency allows for meaningful repetition. Repetition strengthens learning.

TRAINING AND AGE

In addition to the type of dog that makes up an individual team, the age and individual temperament also determine the most appropriate training. Since you are aiming for a team that runs and functions as a unit, a successful driver will ultimately end up with animals of compatible type and temperament that respond best to the driver's individual brand of interaction.

Training must always address the physical and mental stage of a dog. Within my dog lot, I have structured my training for three age groups of dogs:

- Puppies (anything up to one year old),
- Yearlings (dogs between one and two years old, usually in their first full season of training and conditioning), and
- Adults (two years and older).

Many good cases can be made for dividing your dogs into different categories than these. Unless you own a very large number of dogs, however, these groupings seem to provide a workable framework.

Since my puppies are born within a couple of months of each other, (I like to have bitches bred before June 1) their closeness of age makes it practical to deal with them functionally as one group. Likewise, though I recognize that my yearlings are not as strong as my adult dogs, they can and should train with the adults as long as your expectations are properly modified. They will have their speed in that year but not yet their full endurance and strength.

Among the adults a good two year old will be better as a three year old, but he has learned things that the yearlings have not yet experienced and practically speaking can be trained as the other adults. We are training individuals to become a team. If you can keep that in mind, I think it is practical to conceptualize your dogs in these three groups.

PUPPIES

I have bred between one and five litters every year. They are usually born between June and August. Because of the numbers involved I do very little individual training. I make sure that the pups have good nutrition, space to exercise, get all their vaccinations, kept parasite free and are well socialized. I do think it is important that they are taught at least one or two things as young puppies. It almost doesn't matter what it is they learn. The important thing is that they are well socialized and begin to learn how to learn and to be responsive to training.

I have taught different things to different litters. Because I live in a residential area all my pups eventually are trained to be quiet (I let them

Elements of Training

make noise at feeding, when being loaded in the truck and I let them howl for a minute or two as a group.) George told me once he makes his pups wait for their food until he ok's it for them to eat.

Harris Dunlap has said he teaches his pups to come to him, which is handy. He has often said that if you can teach a dog to come, you can teach him anything, especially if the dog is focusing on something more interesting than you at the time. I would never teach a race dog to heel (i.e., not pull), or something that is contrary to what you will ultimately want your dogs to learn. It is important however, that they learn something.

Kathy Christman harnesses three month old pups and individually has them pull a little plastic toboggan with a few pieces of firewood as she walks them on a leash. Harris Dunlap describes a similar kind of program starting as early as three weeks, but only with very little drag and only for a minute or two. Too much resistance at this point can be very physically destructive.

I have used that approach before, putting a tiny harness and playing with the puppy as he pulls a crescent wrench around for a minute or so.

"...puppy yard has stairs, logs, old dog houses, fences, trees and assorted other playthings and obstacles." *Photo by Lisa Fallgren Stevens*

The Speed Mushing Manual

The procedure is well described in MUSH. I abandoned this method when numbers made it impractical, but it works and I recommend it to any small kennel owner. For any dog that is not of a sled dog breed, I think it would be invaluable.

I like to expose young puppies to a variety of people, experiences and physical obstacles and barriers. I want them to be confident and assertive (but not aggressive). Socializing young dogs is very important for their mental development, makes them easier to handle, easier to train, more comfortable in crowds, and better able to concentrate on the business of racing. Remember, socializing means contact with more people than just you and your family. Dogs need to learn to feel comfortable around strangers too. Most of these things are commonly done by everyone who raises dogs, but their importance bears repeating.

My puppy yard has stairs, logs, old dog houses, fences, trees and assorted other playthings and obstacles. I know people that have little bridges and culverts in their pens. I expose young pups to cars and trucks, put them in the dog truck for a few minutes at a time. I like to take them on walks through puddles and over different kinds of ground. The more they encounter successfully as little ones the less they have to overcome as adults. Doc Lombard has a big fenced area with lots of hills and ravines that he can stir his pups up and watch them run, tumble and stretch out. The pups learn a lot about moving and Doc learns a lot about the pups.

By Fall most of the puppies are chained out to their individual houses in the dog lot. They won't be harness broke until Spring. I have to truck my dogs in order to train. I try to take the puppies along occasionally just to watch the big dogs get harnessed, hooked up and take off. If you are fortunate enough to be able to run right out of your lot, stake your puppies where they can watch the teams come and go. Kennels I know in Fairbanks have their hook up post next to or in the middle of the dog lot. This allows the puppies to observe and learn before they may ever don a harness.

YEARLINGS

Yearlings can learn more with less effort from the experienced adults in the team than you could ever teach them on your own. Dogs are creatures of habit, and learn a tremendous amount quite incidentally from the activity they are engaged in and from the dogs around them.

Elements of Training

A musher's task is to set up situations so that Yearlings learn the right habits.

By setting up the training situation properly you can string together successful training runs and establish proper habits effortlessly. Establishing habits is an important approach to training and a useful tool in conditioning. Just by running sled dogs frequently and regularly, they pick up training that you may never have thought to design into the program.

This is how most dogs learn the basics: to pull, to move forward on command, to stay on the trail, to keep moving until told to stop, to follow the leaders, to behave in the team etc. If I have very strong leaders in front, I occasionally will run a whole team of Yearlings, but most of the time I like to mix them in with the main race dogs, especially when they are being introduced to things like heavy pulling, passing, going through water, over bridges or past loose dogs.

If they can get through a new situation successfully the first time, you have cleared the greatest hurdle. You have an encountered a strange new situation, the team has made it through and you didn't have to holler at anybody. If you plan ahead and set up the situation appropriately, you won't have to holler.

The Yearling year is a most critical training period for a race dog. At the same time he is going through tremendous physical development, he must learn all the fundamentals and to respond to the dictates of the driver. It is a lot to handle. Nonetheless, many things that are not learned in this year are unlikely to ever be adequately absorbed.

ADULTS

By the time a dog reaches two years of age, he should be fully trained. The exception to this is some of the training specific to leaders. The Adult dog should not need to learn new things. Consistent reinforcement and repetition will help maintain good habits. His training should now be a simple maintenance program.

The difficult lessons were learned as Yearlings. Most of an adult race dog's training is tied to his conditioning program. With a plan in mind, the season's training and conditioning project can begin in earnest.

Charlie Champaine
Chassis training in the fall. *Photo by Bill Sherwonnit*

Chapter Six
Conditioning Plus Training: Putting It All Together

The basis of all dog training depends on building from simple to complex, from that which is easy to accomplish to that which is difficult to accomplish, from that which is probable to occur to that which would ordinarily be improbable. Any trainable task can be most successfully approached and most easily understood if this principle is kept in mind. Fortunately, the same principles apply to conditioning.

Most conditioning and training occur simultaneously as dogs' bodies and minds are molded into a good dog team. Putting it together on the trail is what makes a dog team. It starts in the Fall and ends late in the following Spring. With fundamental elements of conditioning in mind, a musher starts to run and train the dogs. For most, it starts on a cart before the snow ever hits the ground.

CART TRAINING EQUIPMENT

Before you can start cart training, however, you need to choose your equipment. I have used light 3 wheel carts like the one Lee Fishback used to make. Mine was an under 100 pound model and you should have your insurance paid up and your ear plugs installed if you were foolish enough to hook up more than four dogs. I suppose a cart like that has some very useful purposes, especially for training gee-haw or for somebody with just a few dogs. It did require very smooth and fairly straight trails, though, and then it seemed the dogs were still going too darn fast for that time of year.

I have seen the heavy Risdon rig and that looks like a good item, with quite a bit of thought put into it. I have heard good reports from

The Speed Mushing Manual

those I know who have used one. I have also heard of a nasty spill or two but I really don't know what caused it. I have never used one myself, however.

For several years I used a mid size Honda 3-Wheeler. It had some features which suited my purposes well. I did most of my training then without any help and even though I did have help sometimes, I still have to be set up to be able to do everything alone. The ATC 200S that I used was small enough to horse around by myself, lift onto the trailer or into the back of a truck, or pull out of any predicaments I might find myself in.

The balloon tires and the compression of the motor give the dogs enough resistance to give the driver fairly good control, and the with the motor running and in gear, the driver can really control the speed, both up and down.

Then I started using a Honda 4-Wheeler. 4-wheelers come in several sizes. The smaller ones (125) are fine for smaller teams (four to eight dogs). I have the larger one so that I can train ten to sixteen dogs (I have a passenger when using fourteen or sixteen dogs) at a time and still have absolute control. I give up some of the ease of being able to lift it around, but it has reverse and I use a tilt bed snow machine trailer to haul it behind the dog truck. For my purposes, the 4-wheeler has proved the most satisfactory and versatile.

I run a six foot length of three quarter inch twisted nylon line between the 4-wheeler and my gangline. The cart has steering of its own so I don't need the wheel dogs close to the cart. I do need to help reduce the jolting effect on the dogs when a heavy cart hits a bump or a pothole. The stretching quality and the length of the nylon line acts to soften the impact of some of those trail hazards.

I want a cart to be heavy enough so that the dogs cannot drag it very easily if I have to stop to attend to a dog up in the team. Sometimes you can make a light cart heavy enough simply by taking a passenger that can stay on the cart if you need to get off to deal with a problem. You want control. On the other hand I want the cart light enough so that the dogs can run. I want them to be able to maintain a steady lope.

Charlie Champaine used to routinely hook up sixteen dogs to his VW chassis (with chains on all four wheels for braking control) and yet maintain absolute control. I think nowadays however, Charlie and wife Roxy use the 4-wheeler more often.

Conditioning

Gareth Wright used to use ganglines made of chains when harness breaking a team of wild puppies to prevent any line chewing and to give absolute security.

Harris Dunlap has recommended a gangline which uses sections of standard 2/0 chain in the center line where a dog might chew the line. He makes the neckline with choke chain material with snaps at each end so that it can be snapped on to the center line at any point. (The choke chain material is not used as a choke chain! It is simply used as an ordinary neckline would, but the dog cannot chew through it.) Poly rope is used for the tuglines as well as the greatest portion of the center line. These areas are not usually in danger of being chewed and the little stretch that is available from polyethylene line is a significant shock absorber.

Harvey Drake and Linda Leonard have used ganglines made from conventional three strand twisted nylon rope to defeat line chewing. The nylon is much more resistant to line chewing than the polyethylene or polypropylene lines normally used. Harvey only uses this set up for training however, since the twisted nylon has a tendency to coil when slack and tangle more easily.

If you have a bunch that is prone to chewing lines or you are fearful they are going to bust loose, one of these options might give you enough peace of mind to conduct cart training the way you want it to be conducted.

FALL CART TRAINING

When Fall gets in the air the big dogs know that soon they will be running again. Vacation is over and they are primed and crazy to run. By the middle of September I start cart training. One of the biggest training benefits of cart training is that if you have a heavy enough cart, you can have excellent control over even large teams, no matter how crazy they are.

Charlie Champaine talks about how he likes to be able to drive the cart to one side of the trail or the other in order to force a dog over to the correct side of the line. You are never going very fast with a cart so the yearlings especially can safely learn how to get around the lines, get themselves out of minor tangles and learn that life is easier if they are in the right place.

The primary conditioning benefit of cart training is the building and firming of muscles. The primary training benefit is the opportunity for

The author on 4-Wheeler. "I can train ten to sixteen dogs... and still have absolute control." *Photo by Eric Hill for The Anchorage Daily News*

Conditioning

dogs to learn how to work, pull hard, and pull together. This is especially critical for the yearlings. It often seems that if a dog has not learned how to work by the end of his yearling season, it will be very difficult to ever really instill it in him.

Dogs that never have to pull any substantial weight may do well in fast trail situations, but these are the dogs who will trot up hills and look back at you questioningly when they encounter deep snow or tough going. Dogs that have only run in big fast teams often learn to apply only as much pull as it takes when they are running fast. They seem to learn to apply that much pull no matter how fast they travel. When the pulling gets hard they slow down. Dogs that learn to pull hard first seem to increase their speed when the pulling gets easy.

When conditioning and training of the dogs starts up again in fall time, the whole scene is usually chaos. Everything seems to take twice as long. The dogs are at their noisiest, squirmiest, and craziest to go. Everybody is physically soft, even though they are mentally ready to put the pedal to the floor. The driver is rusty, timing is off, the ability to anticipate what the dogs will do is out of synch and sluggish, not like last spring or even what it will be like in a couple of weeks. I find myself opening my mouth far more than I know I should and ever will the rest of the season.

Pretty soon they will settle down some, and I will get back into the rhythm of conditioning and training, saying nothing unless I expect something to happen, toughening in the dogs, but not demanding much at this point but basic steadiness.

Early fall conditioning with cart is very important to the conditioning and training program for a dog team. It offers excellent control and plenty of opportunity to move dogs around, try out young dogs in lead and toughen in the dogs.

It can be overdone, as can anything, and serves an entirely different purpose than training on a sled. I start with one or two mile runs and progress as the dogs strengthen. I almost never exceed four mile runs on cart. They can step from four mile cart runs directly to ten mile runs on snow. Cart training serves to muscle dogs up, toughen them in and teach dogs to work. This and hill work that will be done later are the strength elements of a conditioning program.

This is especially valuable to younger dogs, particularly the yearlings. Young dogs, though they may be far more exuberant, are rarely as strong as the veterans. Race dogs don't even look like they are fully muscled until they are about three years old, and that is not a coincidence. Strength training for young dogs only makes sense. All of this can be done in a context where the driver has total control.

If you use a heavy cart, such as a stripped down car chassis, the first several times out are going to make the dogs muscle sore. If you need a clearer explanation, grab a few buddies and try pulling your cart around for a mile or two and see how you feel the next morning. This kind of exercise is equivalent to lifting weights. The muscle soreness indicates a lot of tissue has been broken down. That is normal and the muscle will grow back bigger and stronger in a few days.

This kind of conditioning requires plenty of rest and recuperative time. It serves no purpose to put dogs through heavy exercise when their body is in a broken down condition. Light exercise such as fun walks or running free is fine and helps eliminate some of the stiffness accompanying this kind of conditioning. Charlie Champaine recommends not more than two (or three at the absolute most) cart runs per week to start.

Dogs need to get tough but not wasted. They should be made to make incremental gains by working out, recuperating and strengthening. Conditioning is a building process, not a destructive process, although gains are made by recovering from vigorous exercise and growing back stronger. A dog needs time to recover from heavy exercise. A dog which is broken down and physically depleted cannot make conditioning gains, nor is it likely to sustain a positive attitude toward its job.

A little cart training goes a long way. Though I may start in September or very early October, it is a long way to the big races in February and March. The team does not need to be in Olympic condition in November and if you are not training for Rendezvous I don't think it necessary to start that early. I have always conceptualized the conditioning process as one of building or deteriorating. It is a very fine edge to keep a dog team at their peak. And while there is no substitute for tough, you do not want your dogs maxed out before you ever start racing.

Especially in the early stages of cart training, I try to intervene as little as possible while. The training benefits will come from the way the situation is set up. I want them to have to work hard but I won't give them an impossible load. By this time of year I know that every dog I own is a willing worker and will try hard to pull the load. When I selected puppies the previous Spring that was one of my criteria.

Conditioning

If the team keeps coming to a grinding halt, then the load is too heavy. It is better to build on success. You can increase the load when you are sure of what they can pull later if you like, but at this time of year you don't want to set up a situation where you have to force the dogs or even say much of anything. They will have more attitude this time of year than any other time. You can build on it or tear it down.

Remember that your yearlings will not be as strong as the adults and so it is physically harder for them to pull the heavy carts. They will get stronger and more certain of what they are supposed to do, so allow for that in your daily assessment of how hard they are working and the training demands you place on them. As I have said already, we have eliminated any dog from the picture who is not a willing worker. If he isn't enjoying his work enough to pull steadily now, your training time will be better spent on those who do. If a young dog is lazy don't get mad. Accept that the dog is lazy and get him another job. He will never be a top dog but it's not his fault.

I prefer cart trails to be flat or with only very moderate hills. When you are training with a sled on snow packed hill trails, you sink the hook and have control. With a cart, you have to depend on it's weight to control the team when you are stopped. A heavy cart becomes geometrically more difficult to pull up a hill than on the flat (just recall the last time you tried to push a car). So if you figure the right number of dogs for the weight of cart you have, it will be a different story altogether on even moderately steep hills. I have witnessed a couple of different solutions to this problem, each with it's own set of caveats.

Some people motorize their carts and help the dogs out when they figure the load is too much. Some people use their truck to do cart training. This method, though it gives control to the driver is fraught with pitfalls. Not only is the driver unable to sense how fast and hard the dogs are working (because the motor becomes the arbiter of speed) but dogs can and do quickly learn to rely on and expect help when the going gets a little tougher than normal. I have watched dogs trained in these circumstances wait for the motor to surge at the bottom of a hill, actually looking back and not really leaning into harness until they hear the motor start. This is not good.

A motorized cart does allow one training benefit. You can build associations between your speed up cues and the act of running faster immediately following the cue. If your cue is followed by more gas to the engine and the dogs are working honestly, the result should be a faster traveling speed with everyone still pulling and an association between your cue and the act of running faster. If you do not get this result, forget the motor altogether.

My own bias is to avoid motorized carts. If you have to use one, keep the motor running throughout the run, not just when the going gets tough. When the going is flat and your motor is in neutral, give it the same kind of gas that would make the motor sound as if it were going up hill. This will somewhat reduce the association of the surging motor with the dogs' perception of a reduced need to pull.

Martin Buser told me of a trick he has used when training with his truck. He has a length of very heavy chain between his front bumper and the rear end of the gangline. The chain is long enough so that he can see it from the driver's seat and heavy enough so that the dogs have to be pulling fairly hard in order to keep the chain from drooping to the ground. He judges the pulling by the droop in the chain.

The second approach is to lighten the load when the going gets tough. Usually this means the driver and/or his passenger jumping off and running along side. This is only a partial solution. The dogs are supposed to learn when the going gets really tough they have to work harder. Any "solution" that reduces the load when pulling is hardest is reinforcing the wrong thing. Gradually the dogs will try to convince you that lighter and lighter loads are just "too much" without some help.

If you do try to compensate for hills while driving a heavy cart by lightening the load at different portions of the run, be sure to get off and run alongside before the dogs need it. For example, don't get off at the base of the hill or halfway up the hill. Hop off before the base of the hill and as the dogs build enough momentum so you know they will be able to get over the hill, get back on. It doesn't matter how slow they go up the hill as long as they keep working and moving. If you have to get off once you have started up the hill, you have misjudged.

A good dog team will learn through this approach to speed up before it starts up a steep hill. They will learn that since they have to pull all the way over the hill it is easier to keep going if they have some momentum when they start up the hill. Well trained dogs will appear absolutely dedicated to getting up a hill.

As I mentioned this is a radically different approach than that which happens later on snow hills. It is because of the time of year. I am not trying to force anything but to teach through success in progressively more difficult tasks. We start short and build strength, endurance and proper behavior just by placing dogs in situations where these habits will be naturally established and reinforced. Nothing succeeds like success. Gradually bigger successes become easy. Attitude is maintained while conditioning is being advanced. All the time the dogs are learning (i.e., being trained) how to do things the right way.

Cart training is physically hard on dogs. It is the equivalent of lifting heavy weights. It should be made as mentally easy as possible. The yearlings can learn a lot of valuable lessons without applying any pressure whatsoever. Examine your own performance after each run and be honest in your self criticism. You can afford to be more forgiving with the dogs during this period. The season has only begun. Soon you will start getting sharper and so will the dogs.

I think the single greatest mistake that most mushers make is talking to and yelling at their dogs too much. The less you say the more meaning it will have. The quieter you speak the harder dogs have to listen. One yardstick you can apply to your training method is to note how little you can say during the course of a run. If you take a passenger along make sure that he/she understands that there will be time for conversation after, not during the run.

The less you say the easier it is for dogs to distinguish your tone and your meaning. If you talk too much they will eventually stop listening all together. If you have to holler at your dogs in order for them to respond, pretty soon they will only respond when you do holler. The next step they try is not responding at all. If you have to holler to produce response then it is time to correct the problem, not later on when you can do nothing about it.

If you have a suitable trail system this is a good time to review gee/haw with your leaders. Nobody is in any real hurry and you will have good control over the team. No pressure, just repetition and review will suffice.

LATE FALL

Between cart training and good training on snow, it seems I always face a transitional period of very marginal trails. It is a time when fall puddles are frozen just enough to break when dogs run over them, or there is just enough snow to hide the irregularities in the trail but not to cover them adequately.

This is the time of year to keep the size of training units way down, never more than eight dogs or so, unless trails are in really good shape.

The Speed Mushing Manual

I would usually start with five or six-dog teams and move to eight or ten-dog teams when trail conditions improve enough. It is important to keep the speed down at this point. The dogs want to be running much faster than they should this early in the season. They are more susceptible to injury at this point than any other. Depending on how much cart training was done muscles are probably still soft and the joints relatively unprotected.

In fall conditioning the driver has to prevent dogs from going as fast as they want so that muscles can get used to this kind of exertion and protect the most vulnerable joints. At the same time, this approach reinforces the necessity of each dog working and pulling. You have more control because the units are smaller. And control is necessary if you want to prevent injury and train a dog team.

I let them enjoy it. If I have had adequate cart time, they will be fairly well muscled and the small team size will control the speed sufficiently. I don't make an effort to slow them down needlessly except to keep the teams small (six dogs at first, eight later when the trails are proven good). At this point we still do not need blitzing speed. You need to get the dogs in condition by giving them good workouts, and time to recover.

By the time I am able to drive on snow, the dogs have already built up considerable strength. Driving on snow is like starting over for them. They are no longer pulling heavy loads but running almost freely. Because I am never able to set a hook very well after those first couple of snowfalls, I am forced to run smaller teams and looking for trees to hook to when I want to stop. You cannot train a dog team unless you have control. If you cannot stop and hold your team then you do not have control.

Driving a big string of dogs is a little like having an elephant on a leash. You cannot physically control that much power unless the dogs believe you can and don't even consider the possibility of anything different. The control of a big team is achieved long before, when dogs are trained in controllable units, learning the right behavior and the right responses. They are learning that the driver calls the shots. Once an elephant realizes it can do what it pleases, it probably will.

I keep mileage records. Each day I'll indicate for each dog how far we trained, and the season's cumulative mileage to that point. Both Marvin Kokrine and Charlie Champaine have told me they don't bother keeping mileage records. Marvin said, "I just go on how they look."

Obviously both of these guys have a good eye for the current status of their dogs, and that developed eye should be a goal of every dog driver.

Mileage records are not intended to tell you what to do next, however, but to give a concrete reconstruction of what you and the dogs have already done. It is information that may show patterns leading to certain already demonstrated results.

Very shortly the team will be going into another phase of heavy conditioning, concentrating on building up endurance and wind, so this is a very fun and refreshing time that will last only a week or two. We travel at the dogs own pace. If they want to trot for awhile, that's ok, they will start running more and more as they get in better condition.

SCHEDULING & REST

Many people I know like to train three days on, two days off right from the start. I have used a two day on, one day off approach successfully. Still others train every other day, occasionally throwing in runs two days in a row. Much depends on what your most important race will be. I will run a longer distance the first day than the second. Before I increase my mileage I would run the same distance each of two days for maybe two sequences. Then when I increased the mileage I would run the old trail the second day, in that way leap frogging my distances. This also helps avoid a tendency for the team to go out much slower on the second day of a race.

This approach coincidentally corresponds somewhat to an approach used by many competitive human runners, i.e., a hard / easy approach. A hard workout one day is followed by an easy workout the next day. This allows the body to progress efficiently by stressing and recuperating. All work means a torn down body. All rest means a soft unconditioned blob. The best balance produces a fit athlete with a good attitude.

I may intersperse this with a three day regimen (Hard/Hard/Easy), varying not only the distance but later in the season the speed and intensity of the workout as we approach another stage in the overall plan toward peaking for the key race(s). Throughout fall and early December, the entire conditioning program is focused on developing a strong base of fitness. The body will be sound and have a strong foundation to later tune and hone to its potential.

My conversations with Jay Caldwell M.D., a sports medicine specialist, reemphasized not only the value but the relative nature of rest. Competitive athletes spend a lot of time on the brink of being sick. Their bodies are pushed so close to their restorative limits that they can easily be pushed over the edge and be susceptible to athletically debilitating illnesses. Dr. Caldwell spoke of X-country skiers who quite commonly develop a cold in mid season that they never quite shake. A cough and minor bronchitis might easily persist throughout the remainder of the season, with very definite inhibitory effects on performance.

When asked about the necessity of rest, Dr. Caldwell's response stressed that the normal demands an athlete places on his body really determines what constitutes rest. For an athlete training two sessions per day six days a week, one light workout in a day might constitute a rest whereas the jogger who is running fifteen miles per week, two days without any running at all might constitute the needed rest.

What makes the fall workouts a heavy load of conditioning is the relative level of fitness that the dog starts with, not the actual distances and schedule. The days off in the fall are critical restorative periods. The days of rest in the latter part of the winter have more to do with a preparation schedule for specific race dates and maintaining a certain level of conditioning without destroying motivation.

Attempts to isolate the conditions of "over training" for human athletes have generally used emotional indices as a critical determinant in monitoring the onset of a physical burn out. Questionnaires administered to athletes in the course of the conditioning program asking about enthusiasm levels, motivation, and the feelings accompanying the idea of working out are monitored with the idea that the answers provide some direct feedback from the body about it's level of readiness for demanding performance.

Doc Lombard illustrates this principle most eloquently by the conditioning program he employed. Doc lives in an area where he must often travel very far for even a few miles of snow training. He wants to get as many days of training each time he has to make the long trip. He spoke to me once of letting the dogs run as far and as many consecutive days as they seemed enthusiastic to do. When he detects the first lack of interest, he lays them off a day.

This approach depends on the educated eye and judgement of the driver, but as long as the driver reads the feedback of the dogs body and attitude, it should be a very efficient means of conditioning. This method is the rational extension of using the dog's feedback to guide the

Conditioning

conditioning program itself. Doc also allows his dogs to trot at this stage, as they please, saying that the dogs will soon remember that they are sled dogs and start running on their own.

I purposefully do not stick to a strict training schedule of two on / one off. I like to work some three consecutive days of running in and it is important to vary the schedule so that dogs have some ability to cope with flexibility of demands. I plan to participate in some three day races and there is a very real conditioning habituation that a dog's body can come to expect when it is involved in too repetitious a routine.

Body builders consciously avoid getting into a regular Monday, Wednesday, Friday routine for just that reason even though it makes scheduling inconvenient. Too rigid a schedule leads to conditioning plateaus. The body needs to be kept guessing sometimes. This can be an effective tool to keep up mental interest as well as optimizing conditioning strategy.

When the trails are adequate, we will begin the next phase which really starts the serious winter training. My home trails are fairly hilly which lends itself to making dogs work hard and getting very tough. I

Doc Lombard uses the attitude of his dogs as a barometer for his conditioning program during Fall cart training. *Photo by Lisa Fallgren Stevens*

still keep the teams fairly small (not more than eight to ten dogs) and I ride the sled all the way up the hills. I'll have plenty of time to run up hills during a later training phase (when I will be establishing some minimum speed standards for traveling up hills and enforcing response to commands) and races, but for now I am emphasizing work and pulling, not speed. (Remember however, this kind of workout has a very specific and beneficial impact on speed later on).

HILLS

People seem to either train a lot on hills or hardly at all. Most of this simply reflects what kind of trails are locally accessible. I have heard people brag about how steep the hills are that they train on with the implication being that their dogs are harder working than those of people who train on flat trails. I have also heard people treat even moderately hilly trails with utter disdain, implying that their dogs are too fast to have their pace broken down by hills.

Hills definitely have advantages and disadvantages, but I believe them to be an incredibly valuable training environment, provided they are not the only kind of trail that is being used and that the downhill sections are not too steep. You can't train on hills all the time (unless you only race on hilly trails), but for specific stages of my training, I find them indispensable.

The measure of a hilly trail system is not whether it is too steep of a climb. Unless dogs need to have crampons and ice axes to get up, no hill is too steep. The single greatest problem with training on hilly trails is long or steep down hills. This is where a dog is very susceptible to front end injuries.

Dogs don't injure themselves as easily when traveling slowly (with certain notable exceptions, such as feet), but when traveling very fast, the smallest trail imperfection or driver error can throw balance off enough to cause a stumble and a resulting muscle or joint injury. Running downhill will often get the dogs traveling faster than even they want to, and out of control, a canine roller coaster.

A well trained dog will learn to trust the harness and balance his thrust by leaning into it. Normally, the weight of the sled and driver provides enough drag to support this forward leaning. This is the only way that dogs can run fast and still be pulling. That is what a race dog is built to do.

Conditioning

Going down a hill however, it is very easy for the sled to go faster than the dogs. The danger in this, other than the obvious one of over taking the wheel dogs, is that the back pressure each dog has been balancing himself against suddenly vanishes and throws a dog into a stumble. You've been training a dog all along to lean into the harness and stretch out, secured by the harness and trusting you to maintain sufficient back pressure. You have taught him his job, don't forget yours.

Unless you have very deep snow, it will be necessary to drag a heel or two, or an entire foot, or both, skiing on the soles of your boots if it's a fairly well packed or slick trail. You should absolutely not drag your brake. This only reduces your steering capability and makes footing more treacherous the next time dogs go down that hill. Dragging a brake is a certain way to make yourself unwelcome on any trail system. It's one thing to take a fast rolling dog team down a hill, it's quite another thing to have to go down a hill with a groove cut a foot deep down the middle, just waiting to cripple your dogs.

Another good habit to get into is to slow the team down before they actually start going downhill (I mean big down hills where you know they are going to get moving too fast). If you run down a hill yourself, you know how difficult it is to slow down once actually running downhill. A momentum is built up which can't be easily slowed on a hill. The only hope is to ease down the team just before they actually start down.

This is done by teaching the dogs to slow on command early when training with small teams, and where you can exert a degree of physical control. A very calm (using the same tone as your "whoa" command) "eeeasy down" paired with a simultaneously planted foot to noticeably slow the team down will begin to teach a response that can be used later with bigger teams. As the season wears on the dogs will be more attentive and willing to slow down. This will compensate for the smaller degree of physical control you could exert over a bigger team.

Many people want their dogs to run down hills as fast as they can, using such opportunities to expose themselves and their dogs to their fastest speeds. And though it's true that you don't want a dog getting on the neckline and putting on the brakes going down a hill (which probably is a result of having been scared going down hill too fast or having a very real injury), it is not prudent to make a habit of cruising down hills at top speed.

Dogs will lean into their harnesses creating greater momentum going down hill. It is the driver's job to make descents controlled and secure, by slowing the initial speed just before the descent and by keeping sufficient back pressure to keep tug lines tight by dragging whatever it takes, except the brake. As dogs get in condition they will be able to handle faster speeds down hill more comfortably and safely. Still, an ounce of prevention...

If the down hills are too steep or trail conditions too fast, a dog team can be slowed by dragging a section of snow machine track between the runners of the sled. Just a slight foot pressure will slow a team right down. A good size team can be slowed right to a walk if you so desire and gives good control going down hills without tearing up a trail.

It works well and fortunately has all but replaced tire-dragging on dog trails. Dragging a tire doesn't help much going down hills and doesn't give a variable range of control like a snow machine track. A tire will make horrendous moguls in the trail and create whiplash going around corners, not to mention a very real hazard to other dog teams if you should meet on the trail.

Hilly trails are usually winding trails. The more sharp turns, bumps, knolls and knobs that a trail has the harder it is for the driver to maintain a smooth, even tension on the gangline. Skill in riding a sled really pays off by allowing the dogs to pull with the confidence that they are not going to get jerked off their feet. The easiest way to teach a wheel dog not to pull is to keep jerking his lines by over shooting corners, overrunning him on hills, and torquing him around every corner in the trail.

If you are training regularly on tough trails, it is advisable to rotate your wheel dogs so that the same dog is not exposed to the bumps and grinds that will be most exaggerated in that position closest to the sled. Keeping a dog in wheel all the time can have the same impact as if he had a choke chain on him. If he is jerked around frequently enough, even the least intellectually inclined dog will learn that only a fool will continue to lean into harness.

As dogs are toughening in, up hill stretches are excellent places to teach dogs to pull hard, to enforce the need to do that, and to begin to establish some minimum speeds that dogs will run up hills. Hills lend themselves well to training as well as conditioning which gets discussed in some depth later on.

Conditioning

The infamous Cordova Hill, a steep downhill one and a half miles into the Rendezvous, a mountain to climb 24 miles into the race on the return. Charlie Champaine with Bruce (dark dog) and Daisy in lead. *Photo by Bill Sherwonnit*

EARLY WINTER

By early December we are in a phase of endurance building, putting a foundation of conditioning on the dogs. If I have done any cart training at all, I can very quickly get to where the dogs will run steady for about six or seven miles. Training mostly in seven or eight dog teams at this point, I will do nine or ten six mile runs before stepping up the mileage.

Initially I let them trot if they like, but by the time that tenth run occurs, they should be running the whole way quite easily. They are still doing it at their own pace, but I have allowed enough runs at a short enough distance so that the basic pace they are choosing corresponds to what I want to see.

I admit that I had a hard time trusting this approach at first. I learned in the "always keep them running" school and was very much concerned that the dogs would simply train themselves to go slow. But good dogs that are well fed and conditioned like to run fast. At each mileage increase I give them time to allow their conditioning level to reach a point where they can easily run the entire distance at the basic pace. Then I bump the mileage by the next increment.

If I have been running six or seven miles, then I will increase the mileage to ten miles. The very next day I will run seven, then rest a day followed by ten, ten,seven,rest,ten,seven, rest,ten,ten, rest as an example. Much will depend on the trail conditions and how the dogs look. My next increment would be to twelve or fourteen miles. As distance increases so should team size. Hopefully trail conditions allow at least ten dog teams by the time you are going ten miles.

I have a ten mile race (two days) on New Year's day in Anchorage that is usually a blitz race (very, very fast) so I want to have them ready to roll for that but if I have not been able to get enough miles on for the conditioning level I want by this time of year, I will sacrifice that fine edge of speed and continue with my endurance program. This is all taking place in December, with anticipation of Rendezvous always on my mind.

Chapter Seven

Speed

DECEMBER AND BEYOND: GETTING FIT, GETTING FAST

December is certainly the most demanding month for the dogs. Not only are they in their most difficult conditioning phase, but the training demands placed on them also places the heaviest burden that they are likely to carry all season. All fall their fitness level has been building. Habits have been reinforced and firmly established. Now speed and response to driver speed commands are brought into focus.

Speed and how to get it is probably more misunderstood than any other aspect of dog mushing except the use of a whip. In order for a dog team to race fast, they have to train fast, some of the time, not all the time, but at least some of the time. There are many people who go to either extreme. I know people who load their dogs down with lots of weight in the basket or who drag tires behind small teams all the time, thinking that when they get to race day that the dogs will be so much faster because they no longer have the extra weight to pull.

Can you imagine a Reggie Jackson always using a leaded baseball bat except when he goes to bat in the World Series? Have you ever known of any human runner who trained exclusively with weight around their ankles? Though slowing dogs down is important at times (for example, at the very start of the season when they are prone to injury, when they are young and insane, when you have a rough trail) if dogs go slow all the time you are training and conditioning, you will have dogs that go slow all the time.

I know people who take the other extreme by trying to keep their dogs running their fastest at all times, come hell or high water. They do not want hills, tough trails, or any distance that will discourage their dogs from going all out all the way. This approach produces more than its share of injured dogs, sour dogs, quitting dogs and dogs that will slow down like they are in quicksand at the first hint of tough going, whether its fresh snow, warm temperature, soft trail, or any other moderating influence on a dog race.

The name of the game is to have your dogs go fast when you want, not when the dogs want. To run fast, a dog must have the genetic endowment, the benefit of good nutrition, health, and motivation. A fast dog team has to be properly conditioned and trained. Conditioning for speed allows the dogs to respond favorably. Training the dogs to respond allows the goods to be delivered when they are ordered.

There are at least two speeds that a dog musher needs to know and instill, the basic pace and the response speed. Each of these is dramatically affected by both conditioning and training. A dog team that is not in shape cannot maintain a fast pace nor reach further for the burst of speed when called for by the driver.

BASIC PACE

Basic pace is trained into the dogs. Perhaps more than any other aspect of training, it is integral to the conditioning process. It is a product of the way the conditioning workouts are structured and the habit that is built into the minds and muscle memory of the dogs. It is a function of the dogs' natural ability and the training acumen of the driver.

As the dogs start to get in pretty fair condition you can begin to pay more attention to establishing a basic pace. This is done through completely positive means and is integral to the way you organize your conditioning program. Again, you establish the conditions of the situation so the dogs will naturally travel at the desired speed. In this way, dogs are motivated into a good basic pace, not driven into it.

For example, an increase in your team size should immediately increase the basic pace. That pace can be maintained by adjusting the length and frequency of runs as well as number and duration of rests during a training run. Dogs get tired of the same trail after a while. A new trail will usually result in increase in speed. Interesting trails with variety of terrain and scenery also keep dogs attitude up longer.

Straight out and back on the same common trail is particularly boring to a team and will make their pace sluggish after very few runs. Dogs' attitude and the strength of their physical condition will also contribute to the basic pace. A dog team that is not in condition cannot be expected to maintain a fast basic pace. Likewise a team that is asked to go too far will soon learn to compensate by going out slower. In general, shorter runs and bigger teams will encourage a faster pace. At the other extreme, long runs and small teams will encourage a slower pace.

Do not try to alter a team's basic pace by using a whip or attempting any method of force. You may get an initial speed up response, but in the long run it will not pay off. It's overkill.

We have seen naturally fast dog teams that run so slowly on their own that they are pressure driven nearly the entire length of a race in order to maintain the necessary competitive speed. This situation almost always is a downward spiral. These dogs were likely forced to go faster than they wanted earlier than their condition warranted.

This results in tremendous stress and the draining effect of an all out effort. They are rarely given adequate time to recover and so they tend to travel more slowly when left to set their own pace. They have also begun to learn that the fool on the back is never satisfied. He will always ask them to go faster, and faster.

A dog soon learns that no matter how fast he starts he is going to be asked to do more than he is capable of, and pay the penalty of a when he doesn't. The smart dog in this team saves as much as he can until the last possible moment. The team has been trained not to go fast except under the greatest possible pressure and intimidation. The more pressure applied the slower the dogs travel on their own. The basic pace drops way down which brings more pressure and eventually leaves the dogs no reasonable way out but to bolt or quit.

Once in awhile, a team like this will go through a race at a tremendously fast time, all of them standing up to the whip popping and yelling the whole way. This success is like a slot machine payoff that confirms the drivers approach to himself. He is now convinced that it can work. And it can, just not consistently or very predictably and hardly ever in a really tough three day race.

A good basic pace allows the dogs to run easily without mental stress and gives more authority to the occasions when pressure does need to be applied. When a dog is pressured, it can either respond correctly or look for a way out. It is only common sense that pressure in moderate doses can be easily absorbed, effectively and appropriately directed.

CONDITIONING FOR SPEED

Early conditioning on hills was mentioned as a strength exercise. Speed draws on strength. We know that slow, high - intensity work improves speed. But to travel fast, the best conditioning is to travel fast. The trick is how often, how long and how far to make for the most efficient means of developing and improving the speed of a dog team.

"Top end," "drive," "fast finishing," all refer to the kind of speed that every dog musher would like to have when he commands. This kind of speed depends on the genetically endowed speed capability of the dog and other factors already mentioned. Conditioning is one more aspect that affects speed. It cannot make speedsters out of slugs nor Greyhounds out of Siberian Huskies. It can allow the full speed potential of an individual dog to be brought out.

Speed workouts can and should be integrated into the "hard - easy" approach to conditioning once the dogs have a good base of fitness. Never ask a dog to do more than is it is physically ready to do. You cannot make a dog get in condition faster than it is able. To ask for all out speed before a solid foundation of strength and muscular endurance is developed is not sound conditioning (nor thinking).

Not until the dogs are well muscled, have started to acquire a fair degree of endurance and are working smoothly and honestly do I start paying any attention at all to speed development. I make sure the dogs are ready for speed workouts before I get into them.

Usually by the last three weeks of December, I want to do at least half of my runs on fairly flat, smooth trails. This does not mean that we are going to go all out all the time from here on, but the team does need some familiarity with speed and needs to start more clearly defining its basic pace. Up until the first week in December I have been focusing on endurance. By the second week in December I want to change the emphasis to conditioning for speed and training for response.

Speed workouts should be conducted in a situation where dogs can get up to the speed you want to be able to obtain on command. This means training with at least eight dogs for an open class team, but preferably ten or twelve (or more if you are a heavyweight). I want to have several runs with the team working as a raceable unit and get more specific feedback on individual dogs in the bigger team setting.

From here on in you want to define a basic pace below which the dogs are not allowed to travel unless you so specify. This has more to

Speed

do with the situation you put them in rather than heavy duty enforcement of the "law." Usually the transition to a bigger team on good fast trails takes care of that all by itself. How far you travel, how frequently you stop, and your own pedaling can further influence the basic pace the team travels.

It is a good idea to have timed stretches of trail. If it is measured, all the better, you can vaguely transfer this measure to the pace of races you will participate in. If it is not measured, you can still judge accurately the relative speed the team is traveling from run to run by monitoring the time from point to point. This helps heighten an important skill for you the driver to acquire, to have an accurate sense of pace so that you know when the dogs are traveling too fast or too slowly in a race.

Speed work can be most efficient when done in repetitious bursts. If for example, you want to increase speed, running as fast as you can as far as you can once a day is nowhere near as efficient as running as fast as you can for a shorter distance many times in one day.

This approach has been called "INTERVAL TRAINING" by human runners and has been considered a normal component of conditioning for decades. Interval conditioning is nothing more than alternating exercise with rest periods, but it has proven to be one of the most effective conditioning techniques available, especially for developing speed.

High speed is reached for a short burst, followed by immediate rest (active or passive), followed by another burst of hard fast running, followed by rest, etc. The variables of this procedure are the LENGTH of the speed bursts (as measured by distance or by time), the DURATION of the rest interval, the PACE of the bursts, the NUMBER of repetitions, and the KIND of rests between the repetitions.

Interval training is a proven conditioning technique for improving the distance speed can be maintained. It is a hard workout, be not mistaken. Most runners I have talked to always follow first mention of "intervals" with a groan, though all recognize its value.

INTERVALS

The DISTANCE OF THE INTERVAL depends on the condition of the dogs, the time of year, and the length of race that the driver is preparing for. Initially, you will want the bursts of speed to be relatively short (certainly not more than a half mile and probably less), followed by a relatively long stop to rest. I would also recommend keeping the number of repetitions fairly low at first if you have never used this method before. The dogs should be able to run the last repetition as fast as the first. Plan your interval variables so this happens.

You don't want to have to pressure the dogs to go through this. The first sessions of interval training should be more for you to find out what your dogs are capable of doing willingly than anything else. Plan your regimen before you set out, defining how long you want to make each interval, how long of a rest in between, how many repetitions and what kind of rest. Be conservative at first until you understand how the dogs handle this kind of approach.

If speed is your emphasis, you will probably want to keep the speed bursts short and the rests relatively long. As the season progresses and the conditioning level of the dogs improve, the speed work can be longer and the rests in between shorter. Conversely, greater stretches of work with less rest will contribute more significantly to aerobic endurance and less to speed development.

The DURATION OF REST between the running intervals hinges on three factors, the intensity of the work, the amount of distance that you want covered in that workout, and the level of fitness of the dog. If you want ten miles to be covered by a series of half mile sprints, you better plan for a long rest period in between each sprint, especially if the dogs are not in great condition. I am not recommending this, merely pointing out the variables that can be manipulated and that must be considered in designing your workout.

To a certain degree you can control the PACE of the intervals by varying the amount of rest between running intervals. A more moderate pace allows longer distances to be covered for each interval or more repetitions of a shorter distance.

A good pace to work around for these speed intervals is the normal "going out" pace. This is the speed that the team leaves the chute. In a race of any distance at all this speed levels off after a few miles when the dogs settle into their normal race pace. A well trained team will generally pick up the pace on command at specific points during the race and again to finish faster, at about the same pace it left the chute. So the "going out" pace is a pretty good indicator of a fast speed which the dogs themselves have shown is comfortable for them.

You will find that this conditioning technique will have tremendous carryover for response training as well as building speed and endurance,

Speed

but for now make the speed bursts a product of the dogs' natural inclinations. Just as the dog team will go out hard at the start, so it will after a brief rest in between the intervals. (This should all sound very familiar if you have read George Attla's book. If you haven't you should.) Judge how far they are likely to go at this pace and build upon that. As their conditioning improves they will maintain this speed longer and you can adjust the work/rest ratio accordingly.

The NUMBER OF REPETITIONS can vary tremendously, especially given all the variables already discussed. The range may easily extend from four to twenty or more, although it seems most human runners work within an eight to twelve repetition range. Higher repetitions usually mean a lower intensity workout geared more toward aerobic endurance. Lower reps usually means high intensity and fast pace designed for speed development.

The last variable in an interval program is the KIND OF REST that is taken in between running bursts. You can stop and rest completely (passive rest) or you can simply slow the team down to a very light walking exercise (active rest). The implications of both seem very complicated, and I admit to a certain confusion about the specific benefits of each, but both have positive effects.

Human athletes interested in power type events and results use a completely inactive rest whereas runners usually will not stop completely in between the interval bursts, slowing to a walk or slow jog, looking for maximum impact on their cardio vascular strength.

The rest periods in interval conditioning can prevent too much lactate buildup and allow for a longer more intense workout than would otherwise be possible. Use your imagination and feedback from your dogs to design your interval workouts. Remember that speed is not an all the time thing and that interval workouts are much more taxing than they seem on paper.

As I stated above, interval training should initially consist of short bursts followed by relatively long rests. As the conditioning improves the bursts can be longer and the rests shorter. Interval training should probably not occupy more than two runs per week if you hope to maintain any semblance of the "hard/easy" approach.

Human runners I have talked to speak of using "natural intervals" where the terrain they are running will dictate the intensity and length of the intervals. Cross country skiers will do very intense sprints up hills and then "rest" coming down because that is what they are preparing to do in a race. The same principle can be applied to dog racing.

This is an approach to speed conditioning that has been used to train dogs before dog mushers ever heard of "interval training". It entails conditioning runs at the basic pace with occasional long fast bursts on demand from the driver with returns to the basic pace allowed as the driver sees fit. This approach almost always includes the section of trail that includes the finish line as a section traveled at top speed. This is the kind of run where response training can be emphasized and isolated.

You can see where this is very similar to running natural intervals, but is specifically adjusted to the immediate feedback of how the dogs are looking, what the trail condition suggests and allows, and what the driver expects on that particular run with those particular times. The results can often be very similar. I remember following Carl Huntington on a training run and from the gear shifting that his dogs went through, both up and down, I would be hard pressed to say that what he was doing differed very much from a standard example of interval conditioning.

What dogs do without any prompting will depend to a large extent on their physical ability and their motivation. You can influence their ability by the care and conditioning you provide. How you interact with them can dramatically influence their motivation. These factors and your conditioning program will determine basic pace.

I have seen many limited class teams do quite well with this very basic approach, where the driver spends a lot of time with the dogs, gives them good physical conditioning, nutrition, care, and establishes a well motivated and physically prepared team.

This is an excellent way to start learning about running sled dogs and basic training. You can learn a lot about conditioning programs and the temperament of your dogs as they relate to different kinds of situations and conditioning schedules, how you can motivate them and maintain attitude. If a limited class driver had the right dogs and took this approach he could beat most of the competitors he faced.

Someone who has mastered this basic approach can be well on their way to becoming a really good dog driver, but producing a really good dog team requires one more key element, response training.

SPEED RESPONSE TRAINING

A dog team that has developed good habits and works honestly and goes around the trail in good fashion is not enough for advanced racing or racing over 12 - 15 miles (though it will still probably beat most teams). A dog team and its speed must be controlled by the driver, trained to respond as the driver dictates.

I believe an unfortunate by-product of recent specialization in limited class racing has produced over specialized dogs that don't require really good dog trainers and a concurrent misunderstanding about training sled dogs. Dogs have been produced which have good speed and such exceptional attitude and desire to blast out of the chute until they drop, that they will go very fast for a limited distance, without the driver saying a word. These dogs are fast and have a fanatic desire to run, but they never match their short race performance in races more than 10 or 12 miles.

Some are physically limited to those shorter distance, but regardless, without pace control the distance that a dog team can race effectively is limited. Though that distance has increased over the last decade, it can give a "successful" limited class driver an unrealistic perspective of his own abilities as a dog trainer.

A balance between the mental motivation (or attitude) and the physical condition of the team is always interfacing. The real art of dog training is in bringing dogs to their physical peak of condition at the same time their attitude is focused and their performance is fully responsive to the driver.

As the basic pace is established, the next focus is establishing speed up habits and response. This can be built easily as a habit and then later solidified through a trained insistence. The habit can be built upon by employing any combination of several techniques of conditioned responses.

Doc Lombard stresses taking advantage of the dogs natural inclinations to build a habit of associating a command with a correct speed up response. When the dogs are going up a hill, for example, they will naturally pick up their speed when they have crested the hill and are starting down. If you tell them to "get up" just as they crest the hill, you have created a successful building block toward the dog understanding that when you say "get up", he goes faster.

The Speed Mushing Manual

Of course you want to be able to tell the dogs to go faster at times other than going down hill or when they naturally are going to do it on their own, but at this stage it doesn't matter that they are doing it not because you told them to but because they would do it anyway. What matters is that you are building an association between your speed up command and a speed up response. You are teaching dogs what a speed up command means. Later on you can legitimately insist upon an appropriate response because the dogs will know what the command means.

I use two types of speed up commands. The first type is not a command at all, but a cue. When I make a kiss sound, for example, it is based on an association built upon a natural inclination to speed up, but has never had any kind of correction or force attached to it. I would include my "OK boys we're going home" cue in the same category.

The second type is my "get up" command which is a demand from the driver to speed up. This is a command which insists upon a response and after taught to the team is enforced. I will discuss this type of command very shortly.

The speed up command can be initially established without any force or pressure whatsoever by taking advantage of the dogs' natural inclinations and pairing them with a cue. Another natural inclination you can use to build a speed up response is the dogs desire to run after having stopped and rested on the trail. I like especially to do this near the end of a run.

When we get close to the finish (maybe one or two hundred yards) where the dogs can actually see the truck, I'll stop, hold the team down without saying anything. They know they are almost finished and as they catch their breath and see how close the truck is they get extremely eager to run. When the hook is pulled and they simultaneously hear (softly) a kiss and "OK boys we're going home" they will give one last burst to the end of the trail.

I always want to finish a race with a burst of speed so I build it into the training ritual. You can be sure the dogs get lavish attention, pets and "good dogs" when they finish, so getting to the truck is even more reinforcing. More reason why the arrival at the truck is always treated positively for the dogs. They always get at least a kind word. Some teams even get liver snacks at the finish before they ever get unhooked. The finish line is the ultimate goal in any run for a dog team. They will

Speed

be in a greater hurry to get there if it has come to mean good things await them. And the "gooder" the things the "hurrier" they get.

Each run I will start that final burst a little further from the finish and the final rest before that burst is made shorter each time until I need not stop at all, just give the final kiss and "Ok boys we're going home" and speed to the finish. When racing you want a good basic pace with a strong finish. There may be some fast parts of the trail you want to take advantage of and drive faster through. If you have built a pace control and a speed up response into your team you can do this and still come home hard.

The speed up response that is built up through association with natural inclinations is never backed up by any force whatsoever. There is therefore no pressure at all associated with this first type of speed up cue. As long as you get a response it is built stronger with each application. It is a way of teaching dogs what a command means. When they learn that a kiss means to speed up, they can easily learn refinements of this when the cue (the kiss) is paired with more specific commands and then gradually faded from that pairing.

For example, when dogs have built the association between the kiss and speeding up you can easily use that to build additional vocabulary in their repertoire. When teaching them to finish hard you first stop and rest near the finish until they can't wait to dash for the truck, pull the hook simultaneously giving the kiss (they already know this whole routine from having learned what the kiss means) and "OK boys we're going home." Before too long the stimulus of "OK boys we're going home" will have an equal (and more specific) meaning as the kiss and can be faded altogether from the "going home" cue.

If you have ever taught hand signals to a pet dog, the principle is exactly the same and you can see how easily it is done. Once a dog is obedience trained to voice commands (not your race dogs please) by giving a hand signal at the same time you give the voice command, the dog will soon understand the intent of the hand signal and respond to it without the voice command at all.

Older dogs gain savvy over the years. In general, older dogs will go out slower and finish faster than younger dogs, who haven't learned to save something for the drive home and not kill themselves going out. This is one reason you will often see one older and one younger leader paired together in the Rendezvous and North American. The young leader will set the pace going out and the older leader will bring the team home hard. Fast finishing is yet another thing that younger adults can learn from the older adults and another reason why it is useful to run different aged dogs in mixed teams.

TRAINED INSISTENCE

Before I ever started driving dogs I had a shepherd mix dog that was a trainer's delight. The dog was so willing to please that training her seemed only a matter of communicating what I wanted her to do. Once she understood that, she would do it instantly and willingly. But in order to ascertain the reliability of her response it was necessary to command a response in increasingly difficult situations.

When she finally balked she could be corrected and learn that the command was more than a request. I can say that the only difficulty I ever had with that dog was in getting her to finally balk so the training could be firmly and deeply ingrained. This is what I mean by trained insistence. This involves the second type of speed up command I spoke of earlier, where response is not suggested, but demanded.

A highly motivated dog, especially one asked to perform something it was bred to do, will execute a relevant command easily and willingly. It does this because it wants to and finds it easy and natural to do so. Only a well trained dog will execute a command even when it would rather not, because it has learned the trainer effectively insists. This is why some of the incredibly eager hard charging dogs are often difficult to train. They run so hard at the start that by the time you want them to go faster they are physically spent with nothing left in them to execute a speed up command.

A good dog will want to do the right thing most of the time, because of its innate drives and the environment in which it learned. A good dog that is well trained does the right thing reliably, and on command, not just when it feels like it. Motivating a dog means making him feel like doing it. Training a dog means teaching a dog to do it when the trainer says to. Training requires insistence at some point in the learning process.

When a dog team understands what "get up" means, it still has to know that it is a command, not a request. This requires correction when a command is not executed properly and a trainer insisting on proper execution. There is no place for nagging (hollering often falls into this category, as does endless repetition of the same command without any measurable response).

Speed

George Attla
Winner of more Fur Rendezvous and North American titles than any other person. *Photo by Paul McCormick*

The Speed Mushing Manual

Nagging a dog team is cruel and ineffective. Used properly, a training device such as a whip is not cruel at all but is effective. Fewer training tools are more misunderstood and less sensibly discussed than the whip. Yet it is a common training device in use among dog mushers. Most people knowledgeable in the use of a whip avoid discussing it for fear of public misunderstanding (to his credit, George Attla talked openly about it in his book). And it is incumbent upon every dog musher to protect the sport from public misunderstanding. Used properly, however, a whip is a very humane training tool.

Some dog mushers never use a whip and are satisfied with the results they have obtained. Some people have obedience trained dogs without ever using a choke chain. That's fine too. But just as a riding crop for horses, and choke chains for pet dogs are considered normal and appropriate training devices, so too is a whip an effective and humane training tool for sled dogs.

How is a whip used appropriately? First, let's clarify equipment and methods and then look at rationale.

Equipment - I have two different kinds of whip. My training whip is 28 inches long with an additional 6 inch nylon popper. It is braided leather with a weighted core, 5/8 inch at the handle tapering to nearly 1/8 inch at the tip. It is used to create and reinforce appropriate response when training. It will make a cracking noise when used on a dog so the sound association will be made between a whip correction and a whip popped in the air.

My other whip is four to six feet long with a nylon popper. It's sole purpose is to make the whip cracking noise in a race. This noise will associate with the sound the shorter whip makes during training and also create a startle response for a limited time period. I have stopped using this whip for all intents and purposes. As rare as I use a whip to signal in a race, the shorter one suffices.

The shorter whip will crack when it strikes the dog magnifying the impact, just as the noise of newspaper striking a puppy makes the incident seem much more grave to the dog than actually is the case. The whip will sting, but properly used, it will not injure.

Methods - A whip can generate different effects and be used for different purposes. The first (and least important) is a startle response created by the noise of a whip cracked in the air. Since loud sudden noise is naturally aversive to a dog, a sudden whip cracking noise will usually generate an escape reflex.

This can be paired with a conditioned stimulus (e.g., a voice command, a jingler etc.) in a classical conditioning mode. The response depends on surprise and is usually very short lasting in its effect. (Because it is a classically conditioned response, the conditioned stimulus, i.e., the voice, will lose its effect very soon after it is no longer paired with the whip crack.)

Second, a whip can be used as an instrument of punishment in such extreme situations such as a dog fight or biting. Punishment, by definition, stops behavior, that's all. It's applications therefore are limited. There are better ways to anticipate, prevent, and stop a dog fight and other behaviors that require punishment, i.e., something that stops unacceptable behavior immediately.

The third and most common use of a whip however does not involve punishment at all. The whip is used to generate an avoidance response. This is the most useful application of the whip and involves creation of a positively reinforced behavior that will teach a dog to go faster or pull harder on command. If you can think of the whip much as a choke chain, the principal of how it can be utilized may be more easily understood.

When a dog learns to heel, he learns that the jerk on his neck from a choke chain can be avoided by following the leg of the trainer. When a sled dog learns to go faster on command, he learns he can avoid the sound and impact of the whip by correctly altering his speed. In Learning Theory parlance the dog is learning an avoidance response.

Dogs can learn what "get up" means through any of the several methods described earlier, or by pairing it with any previously learned speed up cue. To gain assurance of reliability in the response, a whip can be used as a training tool.

For example: the team is running up a hill. One dog has a slack line and you know that he can go faster. You have your snowhook in your left hand ready to set and your whip and the driving bow in your right hand. You call his name - "Fido, get up". No response. You call it once more, gruffly (Not louder), "Fido, get up." No response.

Never say "whoa" if you intend to stop to whip a dog. "Whoa" is a command to stop. If a dog stops when you tell him to, it's just not rational to go up and whip him. So without saying "whoa" you plant the hook, run up the side "Fido" is on, grab the back of his harness, pull back enough so that there is slack in the tug line, say "Fido, get up" immediately rapping his hind end with the whip until he makes some effort to get away by moving away from the whip. Go back to the sled, pull the hook and tell the team to "get up." The dog has just responded correctly to your command and his reinforcement is he successfully avoided being swatted again with the whip.

You pull back on the harness to create slack in the tug so the dog physically has some place to go. When he tries to move forward you let him. You apply the whip from the rear to direct which way you want his escape to be, forward. You cease whipping the instant the dog tries to go forward. Regardless of the technical term applied, "avoidance response," it doesn't take a genius of a dog to figure out that the way to avoid the whip is to "get up" and get going forward, the faster the better.

Since both he and the team will start up when you pull the hook and tell them to "get up," they and the one receiving the lesson have just responded correctly to the command you have just been teaching. A positive success. By stopping like this on a hill you will naturally be going slower than on the flat and therefore not jerking the rest of the team so badly as if you tried a jolting halt on the flat. The whip hurts the dog but does not injure him. The correction has to be firm enough so that the dog wants to escape a repetition.

I said earlier that my approach to hill training on snow is quite different from that to those encountered earlier on a cart. In winter training I never get off the sled going up a hill. The dogs soon learn that they have to pull me up no matter how steep. Even a four or five dog team should be able to pull you up any hill that doesn't require crampons.

If the team should stop without any command from me, they will be whip corrected instantly because the rule is that they are not allowed to stop unless told to by the driver. In fact, my criteria for pace up a hill is that if I get off the sled I should not be able to run up the hill faster than they. If I can catch the wheel dogs they will be corrected on the fly. These are basic things.

The intensive final response training is easily done on hills because it is easier to judge who is really working and responding when you tell them to "get up". When the team has reached that point in the season when they are ready for this review and training solidification, take them to an area with this in mind. Do not make it the race trail. Some dogs will remember the spot where they were corrected and approach it with trepidation.

I like my dogs. I don't beat on them with a whip. I use the whip as a training tool. It is efficient and fair. I ask of them only what they understand and are capable of performing. I don't nag nor speak without purpose to them on the trail. They have learned that when something is said to them something is expected of them. The expectations have been clearly defined.

When a dog hears the same "get up" that he has already learned means to speed up but fails to respond correctly (when I say "get up," I want to feel a noticeable lurch), the driver should insist and firmly establish the trained response. The time for this fine tuning is usually after dogs have established a fairly good physical condition (sometime in December normally) as well as knowing what "get up" means.

It should take place in a relatively isolated time period of perhaps one week. This period takes place before the serious racing begins and after which the dogs are laid off for a week and treated especially nicely home in the dog lot. If a dog has not learned to respond correctly by the time this period is over, he is best replaced.

Even using a whip appropriately like this is not something you can continue to impose on the team. The morale of the whole team is affected each time any dog in the team is whip corrected. After a week, a dog who hasn't responded is unlikely to benefit much from continued repetition. Any possible benefit would certainly be far outweighed by the negative impact on the rest of the team.

This period in effect becomes the final culling of the year. You can see from this that "whip training" is anything but a year long beating process where crazed and vicious Alaskan dog mushers pulverize their dogs. Use of a whip is really a very tiny portion of the total training a dog receives. It is anything but continuous, but it remains one of the most misunderstood aspects of sled dog training.

It is important to remember the purpose, the impact, and the rationale of training with a whip. Training with a whip creates an avoidance response. Every time the dog correctly responds he is positively reinforced by avoiding the loud sound and sting of the whip. Not only when you might use a whip, but every time you give a command, you should have a very clear definition in your own mind as to exactly what constitutes an acceptable response. You should also have planned your own response to every possible contingency so that no matter what the team or an individual dog does, you already know how you will respond. If you don't know in advance, you probably will have lost the opportunity to respond effectively.

The Speed Mushing Manual

Eddy Streeper
Eddy Streeper drives up Cordova Hill on his way to winning the Fur Rendezvous. *Photo by Michael Penn*

Speed

A whip should be used judiciously. It is just a tool. Like any tool, it can be abused and misused. Some dogs do not handle a whip well at all. Inappropriately used, a dog can be ruined. Denis Christman passed on a piece of advice that he had gotten from Bill Taylor years earlier. Never let the dogs see the whip until you are actually going to use it. Hide it, but always have it with you. Roll it up in your pocket. As far as the dogs are concerned it is always within your power, but the power is in you not the tool. You want the attention focused on you and your voice, not the sight of the whip.

I have dwelt on the use of a whip simply because its use is the most misunderstood aspect of sled dog training. Whether you use a whip or not it remains incumbent upon you to treat your dogs fairly and consistently regardless of what tools or methods you use.

By the end of December, the team should have a very solid foundation of fitness, have a well established basic pace and familiarity with high speed running when called for. The most difficult conditioning is accomplished. Your training is established. You are striving for a peak fitness level while maintaining and directing a willing attitude.

This is the goal, when the peak of the dogs' natural inclinations and abilities coincide with the trained responsiveness to the driver. A team at this stage can walk on water. Enjoy it when it happens, especially if it coincides with the main race you were pointing toward. It is a hard thing to hold on to, and to regain.

The interaction between attitude and physical fitness is a complex relation with dogs. Though many people believe that tough dogs can only be gotten by sacrificing attitude, I believe that the contrary is true. A dog which is mentally depressed is unlikely to be at its physical peak.

Dogs do not speak to you but their communication can be more direct, and although the fitness curve, like the learning curve, is not a smooth one, the feedback you get from your dogs is one of the best indications of their physical as well as their emotional condition.

RACE READY

From here on in, conditioning takes on the slant of peaking for given races. It is important to establish your hierarchy of race priorities. Eventually you will reach a point where the course of action wisest for preparation for one race will not suit the optimal preparation for another. This presents a problem only for the musher who has not decided where his priorities lie.

After a foundation of conditioning and fitness has been established, conditioning and training need to be made specific to the race priorities ahead. This is the fundamental approach to peaking for a specific event. A strong base of conditioning is established followed by a period of training specific to the upcoming priority event. The well orchestrated plan for peaking concludes with a tapering period just prior to the "peaked-for" race, leaving the athletes tough, rested, and prime.

SOME ADDITIONAL THOUGHTS ON TRAINING

Though I have talked about building a vocabulary for your dogs, the tone of your voice is more communicative than any one word. I have heard voices that make your hair curl or make you want to be a best buddy. Dogs have the ear for that.

Select a word for its tonal qualities. Make the tonal quality of the command word match the intent. Guttural tones can more easily communicate insistence than high pitched thin tones for example. As an exercise, try communicating in tones only. Use nonsense words that have no literal meaning and see if you can convey your meaning by tone alone. Remember the distinction between tone and volume. Dogs don't have dictionaries but they do have keen ears.

Over time you can develop your voice. It took me several years to learn how to say "get up" so that the tone itself helped make dogs realize what was going on. Combined with the response of the older dogs next to them, it made learning the meaning of the command much easier for the yearlings.

How effective your reinforcement is depends somewhat on how strong the reinforcers you use are. Take advantage of opportunities to build the strength of your secondary reinforcers. Pair your verbal commands with pleasant and reinforcing circumstances. The words or sounds you make when feeding can take on the strength of that situation when later used as a reinforcer. When approaching a difficult part of the trail, a road crossing or a culvert for example, if you use those same sounds that you built when feeding, a sense of reassurance can be imparted.

Though it's a somewhat different principle, a double whopper with cheese on the bridge made the difference for one young leader. Before the "burger treatment" he was scared and worried about the bridge. After walking out to the bridge on a leash and playing and eating a double whopper with cheese, he lost all concern about the terrors of that bridge. It is difficult for dogs to act on two contrary emotions at the same time. It's hard to be drooling over a cheeseburger and terrified at a bridge at the same time. Eventually one will dominate the other.

Roxy Wright

Roxy Wright winning the 1989 North American with leaders Pluto and Rex. After the race George Attla called her team the best he had ever raced against.
Photo by Paul McCormick

The Speed Mushing Manual

And though I have talked so much about reinforcement, it is equally important to remember that dogs learn through common sense. If they are not learning something you are teaching, then it probably does not make sense from that dog's point of view. A person should at least be able to figure out what makes sense, common sense, to their dogs.

In other words, I believe that dogs don't just learn mechanically. They are complex creatures with inherited drives, inclinations and social responses. But they also have brains and they do think, make no mistake about it.

The basis of all dog training depends on building from simple to complex. Most complex tasks can be broken into a chain of isolatable events that can be taught in sequence and reassembled into a very complex behavior performance. This is the foundation of all progressive training.

Asked at the appropriate time and in the appropriate manner, a dog will do anything it has been trained to do. A dog cannot do something it is incapable of, but will never fail to do something it is capable of if it was properly trained. After all "a dog is just a dog..."

# Chapter Eight
Equipment: The Right Tools For The Job

"A clean run starts with a clean truck."

- Charlie Champaine

As the margin of race victory becomes closer, minor details take on greater importance. Proper equipment in good repair is one of those essential details. The first year I raced I ran in three races decided by two seconds or less. After I lost each of the first two races by two seconds, I thought of fifty ways I could have gone two seconds faster. But you can't win a race when it's over. That is when the notion of detail finally sunk into my head. After an equipment tune up I won by the last race, by one second.

IN THE DOG LOT

Attention to detail starts at home. Kennel management strongly influences the physical and mental condition of your dogs as well as your own enthusiasm. The better organized your operation, the more time you have to spend on interaction with your dogs.

Physically, the dog lot should provide the dogs adequate space, well drained ground and adequate shelter. These are simple investments in the health and sanity of your operation. It goes without saying that keeping a dog lot clean reduces the incidence of parasites and disease. Try to put your dog lot where you can monitor your dog's activity, where you can have easy access for loading dogs into your truck, and where dogs can live in a clean, dry environment.

The Speed Mushing Manual

Chains: I prefer dogs on chains rather than in pens. On chains dogs become adept at dealing with lines and avoiding tangles. It also allows for a kennel arrangement where dogs can see more of their neighbors and get a greater sense of the group. It makes it much easier and faster to feed, water and shovel since you don't have to deal with gates and gateways.

Chains should be at least five to six feet long, but not so long that adjacent dogs can touch each other. I have listened to some people say that it is good for the dogs to be able to play with each other. My experience has been negative as has the vast majority of people I have discussed this with.

If chains are just slightly too long there will inevitably be a tangle and possibly a choking. Slightly shorter but where dogs can still touch has produced unwanted breedings. Even dogs of the same gender who seem to get along famously have the potential for an argument, a spat or a knockdown drag out fight. This usually happens either a few days before an important race or when you have left the house for a few hours.

Posts: There are almost as many kennel variations as there are kennels, many of which are intriguing and useful for one reason or another. Some are suited to one part of the country better than others.

I use car axles for my chain posts. They can usually be purchased from any wrecking yard very reasonably. They are easily driven into the ground with a sledge hammer. They are unobtrusive, fast to install and unbreakable. I have never had one pull out.

More common in other parts of Alaska are peeled bitch or spruce posts. A post hole digger is used to set eight foot posts down two to three feet. A slack loop is made at the end of the chain and slipped over the top. The chain is able to rotate freely around the post. This way the chain end can move up the post as snow deepens over the course of the winter. The chain will eventually saw through the post but they usually last several years.

Various swivel arrangements are also commonly used. Attached to the top of wooden posts, or arranged as a free rotating insert pole inside a hollow fence post, they have the advantage of keeping the chain off the ground as well as compensating for deepening snow. In permafrost and sandy areas some people attach individual chains to a long cable strung between two very hefty anchors or deadmen. This system requires that the cables be attached to absolutely immovable anchors.

Equipment

It also demands regular inspection of the cable. A broken cable in this arrangement spells disaster.

Snaps: I used to use brass snaps in the dog lot. I made sure to put them around the cloth collar coming up from underneath so that the snap lever was then facing forward. By avoiding the metal on metal connection of snap to steel ring on collar, it became much more difficult for the snap to become accidentally detached and the dog set free. The problem that still remained however was the relatively short life span of a brass snap under continuous use. The swivel would wear down fast enough so that it could be broken by a good jerk from an enthusiastic dog.

"I use car axles for my chain posts." *Photo by Lisa Fallgren Stevens*

I am now sold on steel snaps of the type that have a spring loaded gate that moves inward. For a long time I avoided these because I had heard that they froze up too easily. After seeing them function beautifully throughout Fairbanks winters however, (where -60 F is not uncommon) I changed my thinking. The design allows clipping right on to the collar ring. I have yet to have a dog get loose from these snaps and they last several times longer than brass snaps.

Shelter: In the summer dogs should have shade, and water in front of them all the time. They should always have sufficient shelter to get out of the weather. An adequate dog house can be made from one sheet of plywood. A 2' x 2' x 2' house is an adequate size for a husky, big enough to turn around in, small enough to be heated by his own body heat.

There are many things you can do in your daily kennel management to positively influence the attitude of your dogs. If your dogs are warm and dry, they will be much happier altogether than if they have nothing but mud or frozen gravel to lie on. My dogs get as excited about new straw in their houses as they do when they see the food buckets. It's always a special occasion and a special treat. They seem to get a lift from it regardless of how they're feeling otherwise.

The same is true with fresh straw in the truck. After awhile straw in the truck will tend to get wet on the bottom and therefore less warm. If there is any urine soaked into the straw at all, it produces ammonia. Ammonia makes the environment in the dog box both unpleasant and unhealthy. Moreover, it can have a very adverse effect on performance.

More time you spent in the kennel with the dogs is always appreciated. George Attla told me that he makes a point of giving extra time and attention being good buddies with his dogs especially the week after the most intensive training period of the season.

ON THE TRAIL

Belt Paraphanalia: Once I start running dogs in the fall, I always carry at least one double snap on my belt. By the time racing begins, I try to wear an easily reached knife on my belt as well. Roxy Wright tapes her knife to the rear stanchion of her sled. These are minor items that can easily be forgotten at race time. I wear them all the time so I am sure to have them when I need them.

Excited dogs do break snaps, usually when everybody is hooked up and you are just about to take off. When that happens, a double snap

Equipment

is a quick and irreplaceable solution. I've had neckline snaps break in passing tangles. It not practical in that situation to take the time to change necklines, but a double snap fixes the situation fast.

Snow Hooks and Snub Lines: When cart training in the Fall I use two snub lines with panic snaps. Never trust your complete outfit to just one panic snap. If you can tie an effective slip knot with the right rope, that works well also.

Snub lines are fine for hooking up, either in fall on your cart or in winter with your sled. When the snow flies however, you need to carry at least one good snow hook. I started using two snow hooks the first time I ran the Rendezvous. There are some places on the trail where the holding power of any hook is marginal at best, especially with a big string of dogs. Two hooks give you that extra margin of security if you have to leave the sled.

I've sometimes found myself on dead end trails where the whole team had to be folded backward to turn around. As you make these kinds of maneuvers, a hook even firmly planted in snow will come loose as you pivot the team. A second hook planted in the opposite direction has saved my bacon a couple of times. I have taken to using a second hook all the time. You have the additional option of setting a hook on the most appropriate side of the trail to get the most holding power. Yes it is additional weight, but I'd rather carry a couple of extra pounds for the control it affords.

The number of dogs in Open Class teams has been pushed dramatically upward in the last few years, especially in shorter races. Twenty-dog teams are no longer thought of as a foolish oddity. It is hard to justify in a lot of circumstances, but racers are always seeking any competitive edge they can find.

As some bigger men like Gareth Wright and Bill Sullivan sought to cancel any inequity of weight by adding more dogs, many smaller guys decided to counteract that by adding more dogs themselves, much like the global Arms race. When Eddy Streeper won the Rendezvous in 1985 having started the race with twenty dogs, even more people were attracted to the idea. Perhaps in a few years we'll be seeing more than two snow hooks.

I'm not sure where the idea of leather holsters for snow hooks originated. I took the cue from Charlie Champaine. They are tied to the top crosspiece, just below the driving bow. Some people tie them to the top of the siderail. The biggest benefit of this system is that you can put

The Speed Mushing Manual

"The number of dogs in Open Class teams has been pushed dramatically upward in the last few years..." Here, Terry Streeper's 22-dog team follows Mike Boaz and his 16 dog team on the Chena River in Fairbanks. *Photo by Paul McCormick*

Equipment

your hand on a hook without ever taking your eyes off the dogs and the trail. At every turn you can have the hook in hand. If a wrong turn is going to be made you are ready, if not you just slip the hook back into its holster.

Another way of securing a hook involves running a bungie along the top crosspiece between the two rear stanchions. The hook rests on the crosspiece when not in use, secured by the bungie stretched over it.

Sled runners: Since the advent of Tim White's QCR runner system more people are using quick change polyethylene runner material. This adds another dimension of convenience, but not without some tradeoffs. Some of the polyethylenes are pretty temperature sensitive relative to their maximum glide potential. This may be OK if you carry a full range of the different plastics, so that you can test which one works best before the race.

Remember however, that color is not a sure indicator of which density polyethylene you are handling. Having four different color plastics does not necessarily mean that you have four different densities of plastic. Another tradeoff is that most polyethylenes, as cross country ski manufacturers found out, does not hold wax very well. Of the QCR plastics available at this writing, "Downhill V" seems to hold wax the best.

For my money, P-Tex 2000 is still the fastest and most versatile runner material available. It's raw (unwaxed) speed across a wide range of temperatures is excellent. When properly waxed, I believe it is the fastest. P-tex (2000) can be easily and firmly applied and changed, it can be scraped and filled to fix scratches and gouges in the surface, and properly prepared, holds wax better than other runner materials. I have some of the tougher polyethylene plastic on training sleds, but for racing P-tex is hard to beat.

Contact cement has been the method of choice for adhering P-tex. Until recently however this required two to three coats with 45 minutes drying time in between each coat. 3M Corporation makes a newer contact cement that is stronger, sprays on evenly and dries fast - two to five minutes. Life is made so much easier by this product. Whenever applying contact cement, the warmer your sled, the better. Bring it inside, overnight if possible and turn up the thermostat. A rubber mallet and a rolling pin help make the adhesion even more secure after the P-tex has been applied. A sureform rasp can make the edges quickly flush with the runner sides.

The Speed Mushing Manual

For many years the popular thinking in dog mushing circles was that wax didn't stay on the runners long enough to make any difference. That thinking has changed, and with good reason. Waxes Nordic skiers use seems to last through 50 kilometer races. In most bigger races now increasing number of competitors wax.

Both Alpine and Cross country glide waxes and Skating waxes are used. The more you use them the more you will be able to select the best color and type wax for you. Ski racers are a good information source for this. They are most often more current in their information since waxing is a bigger factor to them and also usually willing to share information with you since they know they won't be competing against you.

The primary benefit of waxing is not creation of a faster surface by coating the P-tex with a layer of wax. The advantage comes from the wax sealing the pores of the plastic so that water does not freeze in the micro pores causing a very abrasive and slow runner surface. Though the surface wax may wear off after a few miles the wax that seals the pores remains for quite extended periods.

New P-tex should be prepared and waxed before use. Likewise before applying wax to old P-tex the surface must be properly prepared. Kim Sorenson, the man who made Northstar sleds and who has extensive ski background in his own right showed me how to prepare runner bases. First, the runner must be made flat. The tool for this is a smaller rectangular stainless steel scraper. They are available in most ski shops.

The P-tex is scraped in long smooth strokes from the front to back direction only. We want any disruption of the surface fibers to go with the directional flow, not against it. If you scrape too slowly gouges will be created. You need the momentum of the stroke to make the surface even.

If there are any major gouges in the plastic, light a P-tex candle and drip it into the gouge until you have built a surface up higher than the surrounding material. Let it cool and then scrape the runner and the excess candle material in the process. When you can look down the runner surface and see that all irregularities have been removed, a light sanding is the next step.

Using a fine grade sandpaper, (150 or 220) on a flat sanding block, run the block down each runner eight or ten times moving from front to back only. It is important not to use a typical back and forth sanding motion. The front to back motion avoids the creation of cross hatch

Equipment

scratches that are inherently slower than a unidirectional pattern. The scraping made the surface flat. The purpose of the sanding is to make the surface more readily able to accept and hold wax. Aluminum oxide sand paper leaves less debris. With a clean cloth wipe off the runners and get ready to rill or to wax.

Rilling: Rilling is a process whereby shallow parallel groves are inscribed the full length of the runner surface. The rationale is that the grooves break up any surface tension created by moisture in the snow and thereby reduce friction. It is really only relevant when trail snow is very wet. Rilling is somewhat time consuming and is best done very carefully. Skiers developed this technique also. If it is something you want to employ, I advise talking to your local ski shop expert, since you will need to purchase a rilling tool and brush anyway.

Next comes the wax, hot wax. Any of the waxing irons sold in ski shops will do, electric or butane, it matters not. I use an old portable clothes iron (which is not useable for clothes after it has been used for waxing).

When you have selected your wax(es), touch the wax against the iron and drip it onto the runner surface. Then making sure your iron is not too hot, smooth the wax onto and into the P-tex with the iron. Do this on both runners. Do not set the warm waxed runners down, especially onto cold snow, as it will permeate the warm wax surface.

Let the wax cool thoroughly. Then scrape off the excess. I prefer to use plastic scrapers for this, as it takes off less in each stroke. You don't want to be scraping plastic at this point, just excess wax. Scrape from front to back until you are left with a thin layer still on the runner. Then using a ski waxing cork, old nylon, the heel of your hand or best yet, Fiberlene, a fiber impregnated cloth available at ski shops, rub the wax some more and let it cool down again after the friction of rubbing. For those who know what they are doing, waxing does make for a faster sled.

Sled Drags: Often when trail conditions are such that a driver wants to slow the team down, he will carry weight in the sled or drag some weight behind the sled. One item that is commonly used but banned on an increasing number of trails is a tire behind the sled. The bane of a sled dog trail is a dog team dragging a tire. Not only does a tire create and exaggerate moguls in the trail, create a counterproductive centrifugal action on curves, but it gives you absolutely no help where you often need it most, going down hills.

The Speed Mushing Manual

If you have ever trained on trails where you have head on passes, certainly you can imagine the free swinging tire behind an oncoming sled swinging the feet right out from under your leaders. If the leaders were fortunate enough to survive that experience uninjured, imagine their exuberant enthusiasm next time they see a dog team approaching them.

A far better solution than dragging a tire behind a sled is an innovation I first heard of from Dewey Halverson. Dragging a portion of a snow machine track between your sled runners does not hurt a trail, does not create exaggerated centrifugal force on curves, helps tremendously going down hills, and does not interfere with other dog teams on the trail.

You can experiment with all different lengths and placements. Some people cut a slot so they can use their brake. There are many different types of tracks that give more or less drag. This method gives a surprising range of speed control. Once you try this method, whether it is a six foot length or a one foot section, you will never drag a tire again.

ON THE DOG

Collars: I have used most of the different collar designs that I have seen. Adjustable collars are nice for puppies. On adults however, I have had a problem with metal slides rubbing hair off the neck and also eventually slipping. Plastic slides inevitably break.

The ones I have ended up liking best are sewn, fitted collars with 1 1/4" rings. These big rings allow for easy grabbing and quick changing, even with gloves. Rings larger than this are too big. The dogs' tongues will flick onto them and momentarily freeze during heavy running.

Harnesses: I have a friend who, when harnessing dogs, always asked them if they were "ready to get dressed?" It's hard to think of it without smiling, and its a hard image to shake. One item of "dress" that it seems a lot of people never get around to adjusting is the length of the loop at the back of the harness. An extra large harness is several inches longer than a small harness. Without modifying the end loop, small dogs will be stretched out too much and big dogs will be running into their neckline. Adjust your loops so each harness is the same length and color code them for harness size while you're at it.

Lines: When I made up my first set of lines, I copied George Attla's gangline measurements exactly. In the years since, I have measured the

Equipment

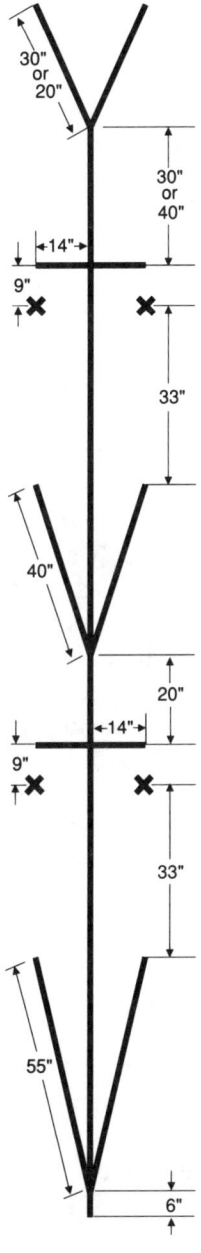

lines of many top drivers. Most are either identical or slightly modified versions of those same measurements.

Eddy Streeper, for example, has extended the distance between each two dog section. Some people, including Eddy Streeper and George Attla, have lengthened some team dogs' necklines. George has lengthened some of his necklines by as much as nine inches.

When they do this they also lengthen the center line by the same length and move the position where the neckline joins the centerline ahead that same length. The net effect is a steeper neckline angle coming back to the dog, theoretically making it easier for a dog to free himself from a leg over the neckline.

Everyone I know who has lengthened necklines has kept the front end team dogs' necklines shorter. There are some tradeoffs to longer necklines. Eddy Streeper says if they are too long the adjacent dog can more easier get wrapped up on the wrong side of the line. Unless you are having a particular problem with dogs stepping over their neckline, I would advise leaving well enough alone.

George Attla's original measurements (first printed in his book *Everything I Know About Training and Racing Sled Dogs*) are well proven and still the most commonly used. They are given again here. All measurements are to the end of the snap. It assumes a harness measure of 33 inches from the harness crossing at the back of the neck to the end of the harness loop. If your harness length is shorter than 33 inches, add the difference on to the length of the tug.

Booties: Until the advent of bunting and polypropylene booties, a dog was usually better off sitting at home than racing with a bootie unless trail conditions were just right. Old style booties did not give sufficient traction. Using them risked a more serious shoulder injury from a slip of the bootie. The bunting bootie, however, changed that radically. Not only do bunting booties wear well and dry quickly, they give traction sufficient to race on.

Not every dog will perform normally with a bootie on his foot. Think twice before trying one for the first time on race day. The bunting and polypropylene booties often have a length of Velcro sewed on to them and this is normally adequate to hold them on.

Harris Dunlap devised a less cumbersome method of dealing with small cuts on pads. Harris calls them "blow out patches." They consist of an Elasticon patch slightly larger than the cut area glued on to a

Equipment

disinfected pad with Super glue. They work very well and impact a dogs running much less than a bootie.

Recently I have used "Skin Bond" instead of the Super glue. This is a product that athletes routinely use to make tape stick to their bodies. Its slower drying times allows a little easier placement of the patch. Its thick consistency allows you to feather the edge of the patch. Most of all it remains pliable after drying and cannot make a pad crack. I got this suggestion from Jerry Wooldridge, a veterinarian who uses this when he does ear crops.

If you use this method, make sure the foot is clean to avoid infection. If you use "Skin Bond" apply it to both the pad surface surrounding the missing piece and to the Elasticon, just as if it was contact cement. Let both surfaces dry until tacky, then apply the patch. Voila!

EQUIPMENT FOR RACE DAY

One last piece of advice: do not use new equipment for the first time during a race. This should go without saying to any dog musher with even moderate experience. Nonetheless, I have seen this rookie mistake made with disastrous results too many times by people who should know better. This includes new lines, new sleds, new harnesses and all other equipment. Incidentally, the same thing applies to sticking a dog you have never run before into the team on race day. Don't.

The Speed Mushing Manual

The author turns the corner heading for home and a "fast finish." (The white wheel dog is "Tom".) *Photo by John Hotzfield*

Chapter Nine

Race
The Games, The Wars

At the end of a race, your dogs and your methods are measured by one standard only, performance. It's not left up to judges, to votes, opinions or values. A clock decides. The fastest time wins. Excuses and rationalizations count for nothing.

I train with the idea of racing. I have a specific race on a specific date covering a specific distance that is my priority. I also intend to participate and do well in several other races, but I am willing to compromise readiness for those races if necessary to be primed for the Fur Rendezvous.

I believe it is important to have a clear focus established, not only for yourself, but for the dogs. A goal allows you to make a plan. Races provide convenient yardsticks to measure yourself, your team, and your preparation. Your goal doesn't have to be the Fur Rendezvous, but if you have no objective in mind, progress will be more difficult. With no criteria to measure against, an honest evaluation of your plan and methods will be nearly impossible.

Dogs in training need an established direction and purpose. The dogs may not be able to sit down and read it, but as a training plan unfolds, they will understand it, if it's a good one. They will understand at what speed they are expected to travel, how far they should expect to go and what to do when the driver says something.

Their performance will be the indicator of how good the plan and the execution of the plan really was. Your goal does not necessarily have to be to win the race, but do establish some goal. Your grasp almost certainly will not exceed you reach.

The Speed Mushing Manual

Ideally, winning races is a by-product of the effort toward improved performance and a game well played, nothing more but nothing less. The object of the game is to win, but the purpose is to have fun. And hopefully learn a little more by the end of the trail.

PLAYING THE GAME, FIGHTING THE WAR

Some people consider racing more of a war than a game, and act accordingly.

I am convinced that the more advanced the level of competition, the greater the role that a driver's state of mind plays in the outcome of the race. Likewise, the less secure a driver is about himself and his team the more vulnerable he is to a competitor's psychological influence.

There was a time when I thought that all the "head games" and "psyching out" that goes on before races was just a product of an insecure or warped sense of competition. Maybe it is, but I have also learned how much a driver's mental attitude shapes his performance and how truly vulnerable that attitude can be to competitive influence.

This is more than "the power of positive thinking" or "psycho babble." A negative, nervous, tentative, or desperate attitude will be communicated to a dog team faster than anything a driver ever tried to teach them. Moreover, the driver's attitude will influence every decision about detail and action he makes before and during the race.

If you don't want to play the headgames you can try to ignore it. You can try to put up a shield or deny that such influences exist. Either approach most often results in simply not being aware the influences being laid out before you. You can only ignore these "psych outs" if you understand them.

"PSYCH OUT"

The race "psych out" is aimed at making an opponent beat himself. If a dog race is so often won by the dogs left at home, just as many races are lost by a driver beaten before he (or she) ever leaves the starting line. In the theoretical world, competitors are beaten by better teams that are better prepared and better raced. In the real world they are also beaten by a driver's insecurity and lack of resolution.

A competitor can try to influence an opponent in any of a thousand ways. Here are ten common examples.

1. The SUPERIORITY complex. Your competitor postures in any and all matters to convey mastery over you. The "psych" logic: "If I am better than you in one thing, I must be better in just about everything else. If you can't be better than me in something trivial how do you think you can beat me in a race?"

2. A variation on this theme is the CONFIDENCE STRUT. Your opponent positively drips confidence. The "psych out" logic: "I'm more confident than you because I have better reason to be confident." If the psych is successful your thinking might go something like this: "He seems really sure of himself. He must have a really good team to be that confident. Maybe it will be hard to beat him. I don't know if I can beat him. I would probably have to push my dogs really hard to beat him. He probably pushes his dogs really hard. I don't want to be that kind of driver. I'm going to try to win but I want the dogs to do it because they feel like it. If they don't, well that's ok. Maybe I should have trained a little harder last month. If I don't win today it's no big deal."

Your opponent would like you to feel; "I CAN'T WIN AND SO I WON'T WIN SO I'M NOT GOING TO HUMILIATE MYSELF BY ACTING LIKE I'M TRYING TO WIN." If you feel this way you won't win.

3. An opponent tries to DISTRACT you and get you focused on something other than winning the race. He can try to make you mad, make you worried or anything else to disrupt your concentration and execution of your plan. He can insult you, your spouse, or your dogs, sometimes through a third party so you can seethe a little longer. Several years ago, just prior to the North American, for example, one competitor cut the locks off another's dog truck that secured his dogs. The victim was distracted and properly concerned that somebody was messing with his dogs.

4. He can IGNORE you to the point of snubbing you. This is really hard on some egos. You can then stew or try to figure out why or plot some sort of comeback, instead of focusing on the race at hand.

5. Then there are the "nice guy psych's." An opponent can serve you READY MADE EXCUSES before the race even starts. "Oh, that's really too bad about your draw," ad infinitum. Excuses before a race are prophecies waiting to fulfill themselves.

6. He can PRAISE YOU TO THE POINT OF OVERCON-FIDENCE. Basking in the glory of your expectations, attention to detail can easily be taken for granted and overlooked. Execution can become

sloppy. Remember your place in the race outcome is not determined on Saturday night.

7. Some really nice opponents will offer helpful ADVICE RIGHT BEFORE THE RACE or in between heats. "That trail is really slick, I'm going to leave out four dogs. A guy would be crazy to run more than ten dogs on that trail." I have seen at least one driver who should know better go back and cut down his team size by two dogs after hearing this line thirty minutes before race time, while his opponent chuckled.

An opponent who knows what you have to do to win may try to suggest reasons why you shouldn't do that very thing. Suggestions about making the dogs run faster or slower on certain sections of the trail because of reasons totally unrelated to the race may be just what your opponent needs for HIM to win the race. ("Hmm, maybe I better think about the race next week and the dog team next month and those young dogs in the team... and forget about this race.")

8. Sometimes MAGNANIMOUS CONGRATULATIONS are not quite as good an example of good sportsmanship as they seem, especially between heats. There can be a subtle implication that being so close is achievement enough, and that recognition by your opponent is reward enough. You needn't win the race. "You've come a long way, baby. It's great to see you advance ALMOST to my level."

9. In a tougher race, an opponent may want you to take marginal dogs with you. When one famous musher boasted before the North American that he was planning to run 22 dogs, some others might have thought they were at a disadvantage unless they had as big a string. I'm sure the boaster hoped to draw some dogs into his competitors' teams that would otherwise have been left at home. Beware of daring new PUBLICLY PROCLAIMED RACE PLANS.

10. One "psych" that can be especially demoralizing is the TURN-AROUND, when a competitor has been friendly and a good buddy - until you beat him. Then he becomes hostile, rude and in general, a jerk. Being nice to a guy until he really starts threatening, then changing colors is big league psyching, and is used only by hard ballers, but it unfortunately is used. For your opponent, timing is the key.

Let us not forget the epitome of the "psych out" victim, the PARANOID. Once a guy has been subjected to some psyching tricks, a person can learn from them or become a nervous wreck, irritable and all the more vulnerable. If you start thinking that everything your

Race - The Games, The Wars

opponent does is aimed at disrupting you, then everything he says or does WILL disrupt you.

Lest you become paranoid that there is a competitor lurking behind every bush trying to "psych" you out, realize that most people do a perfectly adequate job of psyching themselves out with no additional help from anyone. Ultimately it is only you that can defeat yourself mentally. In the end, an opponent can only psych you out if you allow it. The more familiar you are with the different "psych outs" the less vulnerable you are to them.

THE RACE FOCUS

Dwight Stones, an Olympic high jumper, used to describe his method of "visualizing" each jump before he would ever start. He would picture his perfect jump in as great detail as possible. He had a clear picture of how he wanted things to happen. If you can imagine how you want the race to unfold and how you would deal with any contingency that arises, you are ahead.

Roxy Wright
"Race Focus." *Photo by Paul McCormick*

The Speed Mushing Manual

Before and during a race a single minded focus will contribute to a positive race outcome. Nervous chattering with everybody around the truck twenty minutes before the race does nothing to focus your efforts. Concentrate and focus your experience, your knowledge, and your relation with your dogs. Know your competitors and recognize "psych" tactics for what they are, then race.

And perhaps you will win. If you do, realize that it takes more than winning a race to make a champion. When most dog mushers become competitively successful, their heads swell a little and they go through a predictably arrogant stage. I know I did, as did many of my friends. For some, however, it is a stage that doesn't end. Take care you don't fall into this trap.

Credit your dogs for every success and blame only yourself for anything less. Treat your dogs and your handlers well. Aim for a smooth run every time you step on the runners. Smooth runs lead to winning runs. Winning habits, like winning attitudes, are established long before the race.

The flawless run behind a fast, finely tuned dog team is a privilege few people in the world will ever experience. You can only know it fully through your own efforts and day to day contact with the dogs that make it possible. Strive for it. And if the experience humbles you at all, you are a winner.

Race - The Games, The Wars

Photo by John Hotzfield

Do you have a friend who would enjoy this book?

If you would like to order additional copies, contact:

Sirius Publishing
P.O. Box 770404
Eagle River, Alaska 99577